eBay Photography the Smart Way

Other Books by Joseph T. Sinclair

eBay the Smart Way, Fourth Edition
eBay Business the Smart Way, Second Edition
eBay Motors the Smart Way
eBay Global the Smart Way
Building Your eBay Traffic the Smart Way

eBay Photography
the Smart Way

Creating Great Product Pictures That Will Attract
Higher Bids and Sell Your Items Faster

Joseph T. Sinclair
and
Stanley Livingston

AMACOM

American Management Association
New York • Atlanta • Brussels • Chicago • Mexico City • San Francisco
Shanghai • Tokyo • Toronto • Washington, D.C.

This publication is designed to provide accurate and authoritative information in regard to the subject matter covered. It is sold with the understanding that the publisher is not engaged in rendering legal, accounting, or other professional service. If legal advice or other expert assistance is required, the services of a competent professional person should be sought.

Library of Congress Cataloging-in-Publication Data

Sinclair, Joseph T.
    eBay photography the smart way : creating great product pictures that will attract higher bids and sell your items faster / Joseph T. Sinclair and Stanley Livingston.
        p. cm.
    Includes bibliographical references and index.
    ISBN 0-8144-7293-1
    1. Advertising photography--Handbooks, manuals, etc. 2. Photography--Digital techniques--Handbooks, manuals, etc. 3. eBay (Firm) 4. Internet auctions. I. Livingston, Stanley, 1941- II. Title.
    TR690.4.S56 2005
    658.8'7--dc22   2005007446

Printing number
10   9   8   7   6   5   4   3   2   1

To my wife Lani Jan Wallin Sinclair, my daughter Brook Jaclyn Sinclair, and my son Thomas Frederick Jack Sinclair.
Joseph T. Sinclair

To my daughter Bethany Jean Livingston Lebert.
Stanley Livingston

Contents

Acknowledgments

This is the sixth eBay book I've written in two years not including multiple editions of my first two books. It has been a long haul, and I appreciate the support of my wife Lani, daughter Brook, and son Tommy. It has been a long haul for them too, and finally we'll have a welcome break from book writing for a while. Thanks.

Thanks also to my old friend Stanley Livingston, co-author. I learned a lot in our intense three-day shooting session together in Ann Arbor. It actually took me three full days to shoot the color photographs for this book. It would have taken Stanley alone a couple of hours. And I learned a lot about general photography from Stanley writing this book, too, even though I have been an amateur photographer for many years.

Sam Sokol provides software training for small groups and businesses around the country and works as a technology consultant. In conjunction with CloudDome, he teaches seminars on digital photography to eBay sellers. He was kind enough to discuss with me some of their concerns so as to make this book more useful to them. And for that I thank him.

Ken Milburn, fellow writer and author of one of the best books on digital photography, *Digital Photography, Expert Techniques*, gave me advice on preparing the color photographs for the center color insert as well as other photographic tips. Thanks Ken.

And thanks to Rick Smolan for writing a gracious Foreword. An internationally acclaimed photographer, Rick has made a real name for himself shooting for *Time*, *National Geographic*, and creating imaginative book projects such as *From Alice to Ocean: Alone Across the Outback*. Wearing his entrepreneur hat, Rick is also the creator of the best selling *Day in the Life of* series of photography books, an effort that put hundreds of photographers in the field taking photographs for each book of the series, such as *A Day in the Life of Japan*. His latest project, *America 24/7*, was the largest collaborative photography project in publishing history—no kidding—52 large photography books published the same day in October 2004! Most recently he published *DOGS 24/7* and *CATS 24/7*, which can be customized by book buyers so the cover features their own photos. Knowing of Rick's considerable interest in eBay, Stanley and I are honored to have him write the Foreword to our book. And we hope that someday he will publish *eBay 24/7*.

Then too, I am grateful to my agent, Carole McClendon at Waterside Productions and all the Waterside support staff, who always do a good job, and to Jacqueline Flynn and all the folks at AMACOM, including Mike Sivilli, Kama Timbrell, Bob Chen, Barry Richardson, and Andy Ambraziejus who have contributed to the book's success.

And a special thanks to the people at Adobe. What a great software company! It would be difficult to find more robust programs than Photoshop CS and Photoshop Elements 3.0.

Joseph T. Sinclair

Foreword

A picture may well be worth a thousand eBay points. Think about it. With the exceptions of high fashion and perhaps automobiles, professional product photography is unglamorous. Yet it's the spice in almost all advertising, much product packaging, and the like. It stimulates commerce like almost nothing else can, and it's important to the economy. Where would manufacturers, wholesalers, and retailers be without attractive photos to lure their customers?

While product photography may be below everyone's radar screen as an economic force, there is no question that photos sell products, and indeed sell them well. It is a tribute to the thousands of professional product photographers that our commerce is a visual one. Everyone loves photos, and everyone depends on them, buyers and sellers alike.

When eBay was created, photographs became even more important. In fact, we eBayers need photos more than ever. Visual inspections via photos online has become a substitute for visual inspections of products in hand.

Still, in a marketplace like eBay, you operate at a disadvantage. You can't afford to hire a professional product photographer. It falls upon you to do the photography yourself. If you don't take it seriously, the photos that are supposed to sell your products will turn out to be ineffective. Indeed, substandard photos may even turn off potential customers, or even worse, misrepresent products.

The solution is getting some solid instruction on how to take good photos that will sell products on eBay. The book you are holding in your hands was created by Stanley Livingston (a professional product photographer for 40 years) and Joe Sinclair (a writer and amateur photographer). Stanley and Joe don't expect you to become a pro shooter overnight, but they will help you bring your eBay product photography up to standards that will make a difference—photographs designed to help you sell.

This isn't a fine arts book. This is a practical business book that will help you save time and make more money. It will enable you to join the successful tradition of product photography, a time-proven way to sell merchandise.

Good luck with your eBay photographs and your eBay sales and happy shooting!

Rick Smolan

I

Introduction

1

Introduction to Product Photography

Good photographs sell items on eBay and help you maximize the sale prices of the items you sell on eBay. Poor photographs are a handicap to eBay sales. Average photographs will generate an average amount of interest for an item and consequently will not bring the maximum number of bidders or the maximum potential winning bid amount. Good photographs go a long way toward attracting a larger number of bidders and thus a higher winning bid amount. Great photographs often bring a winning bid amount that exceeds the expectations of the seller.

This is an encouraging concept, which starts the book off on a positive note. But let us (Stanley and Joe) use a depressing revelation to illustrate it: There are people who buy items that are accompanied by poor (or no) photographs on eBay, take good photographs of these items, and then resell the same items on eBay for a profit.

Profits by Camera

Joe knows a lady in the San Francisco Bay Area who operates this way. She buys poorly photographed designer clothes and accessories on eBay, cleans them up a little if necessary, photographs them carefully with a 4-Megapixel Sony Cybershot DSC-S85 (circa 2001), and resells them on eBay for a profit.

Of course, this isn't cost-effective with $5 items. It's much more likely to be successful with expensive items where the profits can be counted not in dollars, but in tens of dollars, or even hundreds or thousands of dollars. But any way you look at it, this seems to us a shocking practice, one that catches your attention. Don't let this happen to you.

Who Is This Book For?

This book will be the most valuable to sellers who are eBay retailers. Their eBay activities are substantial because selling on eBay is a serious sideline or a full-time career for them. If you fall in this category, you'll find this book helpful not only to take better photographs but also to process them efficiently. That is, you will learn how to take photographs faster and edit them faster so as to spend as little time as possible with this ongoing chore. With that in mind, we cover both camera work and post-processing work (image editing on a computer after a photograph is taken) in a digital image editor.

Camera Equipment

The camera features and equipment we recommend and cover in

Chapter 2 are the minimum that you will need to get the job done well. That is not to say that you can't buy better equipment and spend a lot more money, but the camera equipment we recommend will enable you to take great eBay photographs for increased sales revenue. When we can recommend patching together a makeshift setup with household items or inexpensive items, we will do so. Where makeshift setups or equipment are not appropriate, we will recommend minimally expensive professional photographic equipment. Using the proper equipment to take great photographs is not difficult, but there is something to learn in order to do it well. This book covers what you need to know.

Computer Equipment

What do you have to have in the way of computer equipment? Not much. You can get by with almost any modern equipment purchased since the year 2000. That means a computer processor running at 800 megahertz (MHz) or faster and a monitor and color card that display true color (24-bit color). However, color processing sucks up a lot of computer capacity. The faster your computer runs, the faster you can get your work done. The processing for this book was done with a PC running at 2.6 gigahertz (GHz), certainly not the fastest available computer in early 2005, but nonetheless one that ran at a comfortable speed for processing color photographs. The color card ran at AGP 4X with 64 megabytes (MB) of memory. Again, not the state of the art in early 2005, but perfectly adequate nonetheless.

We recommend that if your current computer meets this lower threshold, you use what you have until such time you feel you need to purchase something more modern and faster. If you don't have a computer that meets this lower threshold of capability, purchase the fastest computer you can afford. Computers are commodity items today. Unless you want to buy the absolutely latest and fastest, you don't have to spend much money.

It's nice, of course, to use a good computer monitor since these are photographs we're talking about. Probably all good-quality CRT monitors (the big heavy ones) since 2000 are OK. If you use an LCD monitor (thin one), make sure it's a late model with a high contrast ratio (e.g., 500:1 +).

Chapter 3 will cover the software that you need to do the post processing for your photographs after you take them with a digital camera. Although there are many capable image editors now, we recommend the use of Adobe Photoshop Elements 3.0. Even if you start out using a free image editor downloaded from the Web such as IrfanView, or the one that came bundled with your digital camera, computer, or color card, you will want to think about eventually spending $80 for Photoshop Elements 3.0. The bottom line is that we are not talking about big bucks to put together a system that will create great eBay photographs for you. But you will have to spend some money to get set up properly.

What We Cover In This Book

Unfortunately for those of you who already know how to use a digital camera well, we do have to cover basic photography for those who are not so knowledgable. In addition we will cover the following:

- Basic studio product photography

- Basic image editing

- Efficient workflow (from taking photographs of items with a digital camera to posting the photographs on eBay)

You will find that we narrow down exactly what product photography is. We claim expertise only in product photography and not in other fields of knowledge closely associated with product photography, such as advertising or art (see story below). So this book does not necessarily contain something for everyone. It contains only what is stated above, but covers each of those areas in a clear and complete manner.

We have designed this book to help you take photographs that will bring you the maximum sales prices on eBay without spending an undue amount of time or money on the process. Whether you take your eBay photographs yourself or have someone else do it, this book can help you save money and increase your income. It is not self-evident how to accomplish this. Different types of items require different approaches to photography, and we cover the basics that apply to a wide range of items.

But exactly what are we talking about? Art? Advertising? Clear and sharp photographs? All of these? Or something else? What is appropriate for selling items on eBay?

Story *(Pure Fiction)*

Art Colorshuffler, Director of Advertising at the Eatmore Waffle Iron Company, decided to create a photograph for a magazine advertisement directed at chefs working in restaurants that serve breakfast. He chose a tried and true means of advertising: Sex. He wanted a completely white background. The only colors in the photograph were to be an attractive woman in a white evening gown, a white vase filled with flowers, and the Model 510 waffle iron. He called Stanley to do the shoot (i.e., take the photograph).

What's Stanley's job? Stanley showed up with his camera equipment to take the photograph. When he did, Art directed the shoot. Art decided the placement and arrangement of the various elements of the photograph (flowers, woman, and waffle iron). Stanley took a photograph that was clear and sharp with no distractions (e.g., a white background with no unsightly shadows).

This is a simple story. Note that Stanley didn't dream up this ad. Art did. Note that Stanley didn't direct this shoot. Art did. Stanley simply took the photograph. He used his expertise to take a clear, sharp photograph of professional quality. This is the job of a product photographer.

There is a division of labor here. Art has three jobs at his small manufacturing company. He has to dream up ideas for ads that will sell waffle irons. He draws on his advertising and marketing expertise to do so. Once he decides on an idea, he draws on his artistic expertise to make the ad appealing. Finally, he used his management skills to direct the appropriate experts to create the ad. For this ad, Stanley is one of the experts that Art uses, and the other is a typographer who will do the attractive typesetting for the text in the ad.

How much time does it take Art to do his work? First, he has to decide what advertising approach to take. This is a thought process that might take minutes, hours, or days for any particular product. For an assortment of products, however, the average is more likely to be measured in days per product than minutes per product. In other words, for the average product, it takes Art many hours to decide on a sound advertising approach. In this case, the approach seems simple: Put an attractive woman in an ad, and you can sell anything.

But Art had to take into account a lot of factors such as:

- Who are the prospective buyers?
- How well does this approach fit the product?
- How will prospective buyers react to it?
- How does it fit with past and future advertising?
- How does it fit with the magazines in which the ad will appear?
- How easy will it be to create an ad with this approach?
- How cost-effective is it compared to other approaches?
- Will my boss like it?

These are the kinds of considerations that advertising agencies agonize over for days and weeks.

For Consumers

If the Eatmore Waffle Iron Company sold its products to consumers instead of chefs, this advertising approach might be disastrously inappropriate. A better approach might be to use a photograph of a homemaker in a kitchen with the Model 510 waffle iron on the kitchen counter.

Once the advertising approach is decided, Art has to create the image. How much time does it take Art to do this work? The creative process is usually a long one. Just like it takes an artist a while to dream up a beautiful artwork, it will take Art a while to work out in his imagination how the ad will look. Again, for the average product, it takes many hours to create an ad. This is the kind of project on which the art departments of advertising agencies spend considerable time.

Finally, Art has to arrange for the attractive woman (model), the vase and flowers, the waffle iron, and Stanley to show up in the same place at the same time to get the job done. This also takes time. Note that by the time this ad was finished, Art had devoted considerably more time to it than Stanley.

What's the moral of this story? This book can teach you how to take good photographs of products. But this book makes no serious attempt to teach you advertising or art. Those are completely separate fields of expertise about which many books have been written. These are endeavors that take a considerable amount of time. Indeed, as an eBay seller, you can't afford to take the time to create professional ads, even if you have the expertise to do a good job. You would never have time left to sell anything.

Having said that, we also should point out that there will be a few types of products for which you do need to take an advertising and artistic approach to your photography. We will show you how to accomplish this in Chapter 23 with shortcuts that will enable you to use outside expertise to do this work for you at little cost to you.

Goals

What should be your goals regarding eBay photography? What should be the goals of this book?

1. Your primary goal should be to take a clear, sharp photograph (or photographs) that fully displays an item. Therefore, the goal of this book is to help you take such photographs.

2. You also want to shoot your photographs cost-effectively, taking into consideration both time and money. Consequently, a second goal of this book is to help you establish an efficient workflow.

3. For certain items, you need to present photographs that have an advertising character. Although this is relevant to only a small percentage of the items sold on eBay, it is the goal of this book to give you helpful tips on how to do this at little cost.

Goals are dictated by purposes, so it makes sense to specify what purposes these goals serve.

Purposes

The primary purpose of an eBay photograph is to enable a prospective buyer to easily make a detailed inspection of an item. Such an inspection is one of the best ways a prospective buyer has to evaluate an item. Therefore, make it easy for prospective buyers. Provide clear and sharp photographs of the items you sell.

Another purpose essential to eBay photography is to save you time, effort, and money in doing a necessary chore. You have other important things to do in running your eBay business. You need to spend time taking photographs of items, but you don't need to spend any more time than absolutely necessary. You need a workflow that's efficient; that is, one that provides the highest quality for the least time, effort, and resources.

Finally, you need to show items in a special setting (with an enhanced presentation) in certain limited situations because:

1. The alternative is showing an item in a setting that does not fully serve your sales objectives. For instance, a car is too large to shoot in your studio, so you are forced to shoot it outdoors. Better to make the background attractive and pleasant than to make it ugly and destracting.

2. The item is primarily one of visual appeal and requires a special presentation. For example, jewelry needs to be displayed with an elegant, non-distractive background in a way that shows its appealing qualities. Consequently, using a black velvet prop to display a necklace may work better than showing a necklace lying on a flat surface with a neutral background.

3. The item is one you sell in great volume, and you can afford to take the time to give it an advertising presentation. For instance, a vase might be displayed filled with flowers in an appealing home setting rather than sitting empty against a neutral background.

Of the over 25 million items for sale on eBay each week, items that need advertising presentations make up just a small percentage. Still, it's smart to take a little extra care with them when cost-effective.

About the Authors

Stanley Livingston has been a photographer in Ann Arbor, Michigan for over 40 years. He specializes in product and architectural photography shooting photographs of everything from scientific instruments and works of art to award-winning buildings. Joseph T. Sinclair is the author of five other eBay books, eight books about digital technology, and a long-time amateur photographer.

Good Luck!

This book is not designed to make a great photographer out of you. It covers only the basics. But in covering the basics, it focuses on product photography, which is crucial to eBay retail success. It also covers the basics of efficient post-processing workflow, which is essential in keeping costs down and profits up. We don't expect to see your product photographs on the cover of consumer magazines—although that's not out of the question—but we do expect this book to enable you to do your eBay photography the smart way.

2

Equipment

In this chapter, we will recommend what photography equipment you will need to do a first-rate job of taking eBay product photographs. It is easy for professional photographers and avid amateur photographers to get carried away with recommending equipment. We will refrain from doing that. The type of equipment we recommend is, in our estimation, the most cost-effective equipment you can use. That is, it is the least expensive equipment that will enable you to do first-rate eBay photography.

Having said that, we are not going to recommend makeshift equipment that is not durable and is not safe. But where you can safely and cost-effectively substitute common household items or inexpensive items for professional equipment, we will point that out to you. Clearly, you can take many shortcuts to set up a photography studio for practically nothing, but many of those shortcuts will not hold up under more than occasional use. Some are even dangerous.

The Camera

The camera, of course, is the cornerstone of your eBay photography studio. With an adequate camera, you can do almost anything. With an inadequate camera, it's difficult to take clear sharp photographs of your eBay items. Therefore, what we will do in the remainder of this section is specify what you need in a digital camera to get the job done. These requirements are not particularly stringent, and you'll find that most brand-name digital cameras being sold can meet these requirements, including most inexpensive digital ones.

Two Cameras or One?

We start our review of cameras with a simple question, Should you buy one digital camera and use it both for eBay photography and for your personal use, or should you buy one camera for each use? We recommend that you buy a digital camera specifically for your eBay photography. One reason we say this is that the camera you use for eBay photography need not necessarily be expensive. Indeed, inexpensive cameras are in many ways better than expensive cameras for eBay photography. Therefore, to dedicate one camera to your eBay photography is likely to be more convenient and more conducive to getting your work done than to try and use one camera for two completely differently activities.

In addition to your inexpensive digital camera for eBay photography, we recommend that you buy another digital camera to suit your needs for your personal photography. If you're not really interested in photography, you might decide on an inexpensive point-and-shoot digital camera. If you're an avid photographer, you might prefer a digital single lens reflex (SLR) camera with several lens. On the other hand, if you already have a digital camera that meets the requirements set forth in this chapter, you can certainly start out using such a camera before you make a decision on what to buy for your eBay photography.

Megapixels

For online use, you need a surprising modest megapixel (MP) camera to do a good job. For prints, though, the requirement is higher.

Use Online

You need only a 2- or 3-MP camera to do excellent eBay photography. Because we explain this more fully in Chapter 5 discussing characteristics of digital photography, we will not include the information here to substantiate this recommendation. Sure, you can get more resolution with a 4-, 5-, 6-, 7-, or 8-MP camera, but so what? The computer monitor screen resolution is so low that high MP photographs are almost completely irrelevant to eBay photography. Yes, you can take better photographs with higher MP cameras, but the margin of improvement as displayed on a computer monitor is so small that it's not cost-effective. Indeed, we recommend that if you have a digital SLR camera you use for family and recreational photography, you buy a point-and-shoot digital camera to use for your eBay product photography.

Prints

If you also do prints of your products for sales efforts offline, you may need a higher MP camera. Here is a guide to the MPs needed to produce high-quality prints of different sizes:

Print (@ 200 ppi)	Minimum MP
4 × 6 inches	1

5 × 7 inches	1.3
8 × 10 inches	2.3
Print (@ 300 ppi)	**Minimum MP**
4 × 6 inches	2.1
5 × 7 inches	3.1
8 × 10 inches	7.2

What's the difference between 200 pixels per inch (ppi) and 300 ppi? Consider 200 ppi the minimally adequate print quality, while 300 ppi is professional print quality. (Note that prints are beyond the scope of this book.)

Lens

We recommend that you buy a digital camera that has a top-rated lens. Interestingly, most of the brand-name manufacturers are putting excellent glass lenses on their inexpensive digital cameras. For instance, Panasonic uses Leica lenses. Competition to produce digital cameras that take sharp pictures is very intense. The result is very high-quality camera products for the general public. This means that most of the lenses used by the brand-name manufacturers are quite good. Below are some of the fine lenses that various brand-name manufacturers use:

Digital Cameras	**Lenses**
Canon	Canon
Casio	Canon, Pentax
Contax	Zeiss
HP	Pentax
Fuji	Fuji, Fujinon, Nikkor

Kodak	Schneider, Canon
Konica Minolta	Minolta
Nikon	Nikon, Nikkor
Olympus	Olympus, Zuiko
Panasonic	Leica
Pentax	Pentax
Samsung	Schneider
Sony	Sony, Zeiss
Toshiba	Canon

You almost can't go wrong, but there are two things you want to avoid. First, be leery of purchasing an off-brand camera, the quality of which may be questionable. Second, steer clear of purchasing a brand-name camera without a brand-name lens. When we recommend you buy an inexpensive 2-MP or 3-MP camera, we do it with the assumption that such a camera will have a first-rate lens, as most do.

Memory

You will need a camera that accepts a memory card. Most cameras come with a memory card of either 16K or 32K. In all likelihood, this will not be enough memory to do your eBay photography conveniently and efficiently. Therefore, you will want to buy a memory card that is at least 128K or possibly 256K or 512K. This will enable you to do longer shooting sessions without stopping to download the photographs from your camera into your computer.

If a camera does not have a slot for a memory card but instead provides a modest amount of internal memory, it's likely a very inexpensive camera and one that will not suit your purposes.

A word of warning: When you go to buy a larger memory card for your camera, make sure that you are buying exactly what the camera requires. There are a half-dozen different types of memory cards, and they are all incompatible.

Macro Capability

You will want to look at the specifications for the camera you're considering buying to make sure that it has good macro capability. Macro photography is simply taking closeup photographs and photographs of very small items. Fortunately, most inexpensive digital cameras, and even some expensive ones, have excellent macro capability.

If what you sell on eBay is general merchandise, you will need a macro capability sooner or later. If you sell jewelry, you will use the macro capability all the time. If all you sell is automobiles, you may never need the macro capability. So the macro capability of a digital camera as a requirement for good eBay photography depends on exactly what you're selling. But in our judgment, everybody will need macro capability sooner or later.

One way to judge the macro capability of a digital camera is by finding out how close a lens can get to an object and still photograph it sharply. That might be anywhere from one inch to twenty inches. The closer, you can get to the subject and still take a photograph in focus, the better the macro capability of the camera. But every lens is different. For instance, if you are using a zoom lens and the camera cannot get closer than 18 inches from the product being photographed, the macro capability with the zoom set at wide angle may not be very good. Yet, with the zoom set at the telescopic setting, the macro capability of the camera might be adequate. So it pays to look at the specifications (and online reviews) of the camera to determine whether, in fact, the camera has good macro capability.

For most purposes, use the longest focal lengh of your zoom lens (i.e., telephoto) for macro photography.

LCD Screen

Virtually every digital camera has an LCD screen, so we don't have to recommend this as one of the requirements. We should point out, however, that you will probably use the LCD screen to frame your products in your eBay photography much more often than using the camera's viewfinder. Therefore, the larger the LCD screen, the easier you can use it as a substitute for the viewfinder. In 2004, the camera industry introduced cameras with large LCD screens (e.g., two inches or more). In 2005, there seems to be a trend toward larger LCD screens on cameras. So, by buying a late-model camera, you can find one with a larger LCD screen, which may make your eBay photography more efficient.

Some of the more expensive cameras have an articulating LCD screen. That means you can actually move the screen in several different positions. This capability can come in handy for certain types of product photography. However, unless you need such a capability for a specific purpose, it's probably not worth the extra money to buy a more expensive camera.

Check the Sharpness

You can switch most LCD screens into a magnification mode. This is useful for taking a closer look at a portion of a photograph. Moreover, it's a great way to more accurately check the sharpness of a photograph you've taken.

Zoom Lens

Although we have done some great eBay photography with inexpensive, fixed focal length digital cameras, we recommend a zoom lens for your eBay photography. A zoom lens enables you to easily go from wide angle to telephoto all in one lens. A zoom lens is simply more flexible and more efficient to use. There are few fixed focal length cameras still being sold, so getting an inexpensive digital camera with a zoom lens is not a big deal. But it is something you should insist on when you shop for a digital camera.

Incidentally, pay attention only to the optical zoom capability of a digital camera. The electronic zoom capability does not provide high enough quality for eBay photography.

Depth of Field

Depth of field is the zone in which an item being photographed is in focus. For instance, if you photograph a car from the front, the front could be in focus but the rear end could be out of focus. That would indicate a depth of field that is too narrow to take the photograph.

How can you change the depth of field? Close down the aperture by setting a higher f-stop for the lens (see Chapter 4 for more information). This will increase the depth of field so that the entire limousine will be in focus.

One of the differences between a wide angle lens and a telephoto lens is the inherent depth of field. A telephoto lens has a shallow (narrow) depth of field. A wide angle lens has a much greater depth of field. Consequently, with a zoom lens, you could try bringing the entire limousine into focus just by changing the zoom lens to its wide angle setting.

Wide Angle

The wide angle end of a zoom lens is useful because it allows you to shoot objects close up that would not otherwise fit in the frame. Unfortunately, a wide angle lens provides considerably more distortion the closer it gets to something (see Photo 1). When using this handy lens, you will want to keep your distance as much as possible. A wide angle lens can be more tricky to use for macro (closeup) work than a telephoto due to possible distortion.

Still, a wide angle lens photograph provides you with a feeling of depth and realism so long as you don't let the distortion get out of control. It also provides a considerable depth of field.

Telephoto

The telephoto end of a zoom lens comes in handy for shooting things out of reach. It tends to compress and flatten an image rather than provide a feeling of depth (see Photo 2). Distortion is not usually a problem. A telephoto lens provides a narrow depth of field, which can be a detriment to macro work, particularly for an item with a deep dimension. But a telephoto lens is otherwise useful for macro work.

Size

The nice thing about point-and-shoot digital cameras is that they're small and light. They don't require a lot of strength to muscle around. Although this is not a prime consideration, it is one more reason to buy a point-and-shoot digital camera.

Manual Controls

It is important to have manual controls on your cameras. Many inexpensive digital cameras are completely automatic and do not enable a photographer to manually control the camera. This can be a real handicap in many situations for your eBay photography. The more manual controls you can have the better. You may not use them at first, but after you learn more about photography, you will invariably want more manual control.

There are various degrees of manual control. Some cameras let you set everything. Other cameras give you limited controls, such as aperture priority. In other words, they enable you to make one setting manually but not others. This is probably OK for most eBay photography. A list of the minimum settings you will want to control on the camera are:

- White balance (see Chapter 5)
- ISO (see Chapter 4)

- Aperture priority (see Chapter 4)
- Shutter priority (see Chapter 4)
- Flash strength (see below)
- Incremental exposure adjustment (see below)

If you can manually control the above settings in a digital camera, you will be able to take better eBay photographs in many more situations than if the camera makes all the settings automatically for you. You can read more about this in Chapter 4.

Accessory Attachment

It is desirable to have a screw thread on the front of the lens so that you can attach such things as lens hoods, filters, and closeup lenses. Unfortunately, most inexpensive digital point and shoot cameras do not have screw threads on their lenses. Some cameras instead have the capability to screw in a tube at the base of the lens. The other end of the tube provides the screw threads for the accessories mentioned.

A screw thread is not crucial to eBay photography, but it might come in handy from time to time in special situations.

Auto Focus

Automatic focus works pretty well on most digital cameras and is actually a time-saver for eBay photography. Some cameras auto focus better than others, but most seem to work well enough. If you can't get good focus the first time around, you can always refocus to get a sharper image. Sometimes you might have to refocus more than once. On the whole, however, auto focus is a boon to eBay photography.

One can argue that you should have a manual-focus capability in addition to auto focus in your camera. It never hurts to have more control when you're doing photography. For most eBay photography, however, focusing well should not pose a problem. In fact, manual focusing tends to be slower and often less accurate than auto focusing, unless the camera is a digital SLR.

Unfortunately, when you are doing macro photography, focus becomes a very crucial issue. With macro photography, it is more difficult to get the focus just right than it is with other photography. With that in mind, if the main part of your work will be macro photography, you may want to make sure that you use a digital camera that enables manual focusing. These tend to be the more expensive digital cameras. Having said that, we found that we could take photographs of objects of almost any size with auto focus. There are photographic techniques we cover later in the book that make auto focus or macro photography less of a problem.

Light Metering

All digital cameras use light metering to set the exposure. Some light metering is better than others. The more expensive the camera, the better the metering. Nonetheless, metering is not such an important issue.

First, if the metering is off and you take an overexposed or underexposed shot, you will see that when you review the photograph on the camera's LCD screen. Then you can re-shoot the photograph without wasting too much time. This of course is something you can't do with film. Second, in most situations for eBay photography, you will control the lighting. The lighting should be very good for the products you shoot, as you will learn in Chapter 6. Therefore, the light meter will not have to interpret any complex lighting situations. Even the light meters in inexpensive cameras should be able to set the exposure with a high degree of accuracy.

On the other hand, if you are shooting photographs of items such as lawn mowers and cars, which are usually outside, it might be worth your while to buy a camera known to have excellent light metering. It is in these outdoor situations where you are most likely to have complex lighting that the meter will have to interpret competently. Whether or not the camera has exceptional quality light metering is usually something you can find out by reading camera reviews.

Exposure Adjustment

You will need an incremental exposure adjustment. The capability to underexpose or overexpose in increments of one-half or one-third of a stop (see Chapter 4 for explanation of a stop) is essential to successful product photography. The camera you buy should have this capability.

Flash

Virtually all digital cameras come with a built-in flash. We do not advocate that you use a flash for your product photography. Flash photography is such a complex endeavor that we could devote an entire separate book to it. Furthermore, it is not necessary or desirable for product photography.

In fact, studio lighting is better and more efficient for eBay product photography. Thus, the quality of the flash is not so important, nor is it important to have a flash attachment mount (hot shoe) on your digital camera for an external flash.

That is not to say that you will not use your flash occasionally for eBay photography. The flash can be very handy for fill-in lighting even with strong studio lights. But in that case, the flash is just playing a minor role, and virtually any flash will do.

What you do want in a built-in flash is the capability to control its strength. Since you will use it primarily as a fill-in flash, you need to be able to set it on a reduced strength. Some digital cameras feature Low, Medium, and Strong flash settings. Some feature Fill-in and Strong flash settings. A camera that doesn't feature a control for the strength of the flash is not as suitable for eBay photography as one that does.

Tripod Attachment

Most digital cameras have a screw hole on the bottom for attaching the camera to a tripod. We consider a tripod essential to eBay photography, and without the screw hole to attach to the tripod, you will be forced to hold the camera when taking photographs. Moreover, you will need to attach a plate to the bottom of the camera for a quick release system (covered below). If the plate covers any functions on the bottom of the camera, such as the door to the battery compartment, you may have to remove the plate every time you have to use such a function. This can be very inconvenient.

Power Cord

Digital cameras work on batteries. Some also work on power cords (plus a transformer). If you can use a power cord, you don't have the expense of batteries. This is a particularly important feature if you shoot a lot of photographs every day.

Remote Control or Self-Timer

When you use a tripod, the goal is to steady the camera so that the photograph will be sharp. Nonetheless, the act of pushing the shutter release will jar the camera ever so slightly, possibly resulting in an unsharp photograph. There are two ways to avoid this.

First, you can use the self-timer, if the camera has one. The camera triggers the shutter release itself without a jar, and the photograph will be sharp. Second, you can use the remote control, if the camera has one. Remotes are either an electronic cord that connects to the camera or an infrared device that controls the camera. In either case, you can trigger the shutter release without a jar to the camera.

Note that using a self-timer increases the amount of time you will spend shooting your eBay items, unless you can set the self-timer to five seconds or under. If you shoot only a few photographs a day, this will not be a prime consideration. If you shoot several hours each day, you will save a lot of time and frustration by using a remote control instead of a self-timer.

If you absolutely cannot use a remote release or self-timer, hold the camera firmly between your thumb and index finger, with your thumb on the underside to hold the camera steady and your index finger on the shutter release. This will cause the least movement.

Download Connection

A USB download connection has become the standard. Some older cameras may have another means of connecting the camera to your computer in order to download the photographs. Avoid such cameras. USB makes downloading quick and easy. The newer the camera and the newer your computer, the better USB will work.

USB 1.1 is the original standard. USB 2.0 is the most recent standard and is forty times faster than USB 1.1. Again, if you have a large volume of eBay work, make sure you get a camera with a USB 2.0 connection. It will save you time.

FireWire is a fast way to download too, if you have FireWire capability in both your camera and your computer.

In the alternative, you can remove the memory card from the camera and use a USB card reader or FireWire card reader to download the photographs to your computer.

Numbering Control

You need to set your digital camera so that it numbers photographs in perpetual sequence even after the memory card has been erased. This ensures that every photograph you take will have a unique file name. This can be important for your file naming system (see Chapter 20).

What Models?

OK, let's get to the point. What brands and models do we recommend? We will make a bold statement and say that almost any brand-name digital camera with the features mentioned in this chapter sold during or since 2000 is probably just fine for your eBay product photography. To prove the point, Joe used a 2-MP Olympus C-2020 camera (circa 2000) to shoot most of the color demonstration photographs for this book. You could buy a used Olympus C-2020 on eBay in the spring of 2005 for about $150. A comparable Olympus camera the, 6-MP C-60 (first on the market in 2004), cost about $280 new in the spring of 2005.

No, we're not recommending Olympus or any other brand. We think it's safe to say that the emerging high quality of consumer and professional digital cameras since 2000 has surprised everyone, amateurs and professionals alike. With brand-name digital cameras, it's hard to go wrong.

Other Requirements

If you read any book on photography, you will find a long list of requirements that the author recommends you get in the camera you choose. Such a list will be different from the list in this book. The list in this book is specifically for eBay photography and no other use. If your camera comes with the features that we've specified, you will be able to do a first-rate job of photographing your eBay items.

Certainly there are many other desirable features in a digital camera that you will want to have if you are using the camera for something besides eBay product photography. As we have already stated in this chapter, though, we do not recommend that you use your eBay photography camera for other uses but rather keep it set up in the studio for your immediate and efficient use every day. Therefore, all the other features you might desire for a family or recreational camera are irrelevant to your eBay photography.

Other Equipment

In this section, we will recommend what other equipment you will need for your photography studio, keeping in mind that such equipment must be cost-effective. Cost-effectiveness is a matter of opinion. We will not recommend a makeshift apparatus that is likely to fall apart with heavy use. Neither will we recommend something that might work well under your watchful eye but then set your studio on fire when you leave to answer a phone call. Hence, we believe that there is a certain minimum amount of professional equipment that you should purchase for your studio, and we will recommend the least expensive professional equipment that will provide you with the durability and safety you need to do your eBay photography every day. In addition, we will recommend a list of household items that will come in handy for enabling your photography production line to handle a smooth flow of photographs.

Lighting

Professional lighting equipment is a must for studio product photography, but it isn't necessarily expensive. See Chapter 6 for more information on photography studio lighting.

Tripod

A tripod is an essential piece of equipment for high-quality product photography. For a digital camera, a tripod such as a Manfrotto 734B (3.1 lbs.), designed for digital cameras, is great for general photography (about $110). It comes with an inexpensive but perfectly adequate ball head (value about $40), which provides convenience and efficiency for your work. However, this is a lightweight tripod intended for use by a photographer on the move. If you already have a heavier, good-quality tripod with an adequate ball head, use that. You might find a heavier tripod more appropriate for strictly studio work.

It is very convenient to be able to separate your camera from the tripod without unscrewing it. That requires a plate attached to the camera, and a clamp affixed to the tripod (a quick-release system). Professional plates and clamps are expensive and heavy duty, designed to hold cameras up to 25 pounds. They are overkill for digital cameras. Stanley has used them for 40 years and would use no other. On the other hand, Joe thinks that the Manfrotto 384 Dove Tail Rapid Connect Adaptor and plate (about $45) works very well and is very secure, particularly for lightweight digital cameras.

Less expensive tripods and quick-release devices than those mentioned are available and may also be adequate. If you use inexpensive tripod equipment, make sure it's sturdy. Quick-release devices must clamp tightly and securely.

Neutral Background

A neutral and seamless background is appropriate for product photography to ensure that nothing in the photograph distracts from the product. A roll of seamless background paper is a convenient and inexpensive means of creating such a background. See Chapter 6.

Shades for Your Windows

As you will learn in Chapter 6, daylight may not be welcome in your studio. In addition, if you shoot items indoors in place with outside light, you may need to diffuse the outside light when the sun is beaming in. You can use window shades to block light or diffuse light. You need to keep window shades in mind when planning your studio.

Sell Your Equipment

If you have film camera equipment that you don't think you will use in the future, sell it as soon as possible. In June 2003 Joe sold his Olympus OM-4 (film camera) and four lenses for a great price on eBay. With the camera market transforming from film to digital, you can't sell your film equipment too soon. Whether you can still get a good price is questionable.

In fact, if you have outdated digital camera equipment (pre-2000), you may want to sell it to get a digital camera with updated features. Don't panic, however. Joe took most of the product photographs for this book with a 2-MP Olympus C-2020 (circa 2000) and got perfectly acceptable product photographs.

eBay has a Cameras Selling Center (*http://ebay.com/sellmycamera*), which may prove useful in selling your camera equipment. Visit it. Over a billion dollars in camera equipment was sold on eBay in 2004, and there's probably not a better place to sell.

Buy Your Equipment

Obviously, eBay also offers you a great place to buy the camera equipment and supplies you need to take great product photographs. Try the eBay Digital Camera Buying Guide (*http://pages.ebay.com/buy/camerasphoto/digitalguide*).

Perhaps not so obviously, Froogle also provides places to shop. I can often find camera equipment for lower prices using Froogle (or Google) than eBay. It's worth your time to try both to find the best deal.

The trick to finding good deals on good equipment is to know the brands, model numbers, and specifications. You can find these in photographic supply catalogs or in photography magazines. If you know the brand and model number of a set of lights you want to buy, you have a much better chance of finding them at a good price.

Photography supply catalogs also provide you a great place to buy equipment and supplies that are not consumer products. Check your local photographic supply store too. There is one in every major town or city.

See Appendix III for a list of sources both online and offline where you can find photographic equipment and supplies.

_3_

Software

The software programs you need for digital photography are an image editor and an archive viewer. You need the image editor to tune up your digital photographs just a little, if necessary, before you put them in your eBay auction ad. It doesn't have to take much time, and it's definitely worth the effort when needed. The good news is that there are dozens and dozens of image editors that meet the requirements we set forth in this chapter. If you purchased one or otherwise obtained one during or after 2003, it probably has everything that you need.

Note that we will show you how to take digital photographs that require little, if any, tuning up. Tuning up your photographs after you take them is called *post-processing*. Being adept at post-processing is great, but if you can avoid post-processing, you can work more cost-effectively.

You need to store your photographs someplace. Although naming your photographs is important for keeping track of them, viewing them in an album or catalog program (archive program) makes it easier to keep track of them. After all, when you view them, you can see what they are. So between being able to view them and using intelligent file naming, as covered in Chapter 20, you should be able to keep yourself and your eBay photography reasonably organized so as not to waste a lot of time. Thus, an archive viewer that will enable you to see your digital photograph files is a very important component of your post-processing.

Image Editor

An image editor typically displays a digital photograph and enables you to manipulate it and change it. When you make a change to it, it immediately displays that change so that you can see what you have done. It also allows you to go back and reverse the change if you don't like what you see. Thus, we say that you edit an image in real time because you see what you're getting immediately. Here's a list of things that an image editor needs to be able to do:

1. Process batches of files

2. Crop

3. Adjust brightness and contrast

4. Adjust levels (optional)

5. Adjust saturation

6. Resize

7. Sharpen

Each of these capabilities is an important part of processing your eBay product photographs. We strongly recommend, however, that you don't go any further than this. Most inexpensive image editors will enable you to do more. And expensive image editors will enable you to do much more. But doing more entails spending considerable extra time for little additional gain in quality. Such additional processing is not cost-effective, and therefore has no place in the lives of busy eBay businesspeople.

Batch Processing

Batch processing is simply applying exactly the same post-processing to multiple files (photographs) at the same time. This is crucial to achieving efficiency in your post-processing. You need to understand which procedures accommodate batch processing, which accommodate adjustments with a high percentage of success, and which do not accommodate batch processing at all.

Cropping

You crop to eliminate excess space around the product you photograph. This is a process not easily susceptible to batch processing. You usually need to crop each photograph individually. Although you need the capability to crop, it's better to take photographs with the product filling the frame so that cropping isn't required.

Brightness and Contrast

Brightness and contrast are basic adjustments you can use to potentially make your photographs look better. We recommend that you decrease the brightness a little and boost the contrast a modest amount. This seems to work for 80 percent of the photographs that require post-processing. Thus, you can adjust brightness and contrast in batch processing. Nonetheless, you will need to custom adjust the brightness and contrast for the 20 percent of photographs for which the standard adjustments don't work.

It is better to take photographs that don't need post-processing. In a studio, you have control over the lighting, and you can experiment to find a way to take photographs that require no adjustments for brightness and contrast.

Levels

Levels are adjustments that Adobe provides in Photoshop Elements 3.0. Adjusting the levels does a better job of making a photograph look better in most cases than adjusting brightness and contrast. Although they are not mutually exclusive, you don't need to do both for most photographs. Adjust the levels if you use Photoshop Elements. Otherwise adjust brightness and contrast.

When you adjust levels, you can do it automatically for all colors at the same time or do it for each individual color (red, green, blue) separately, one at a time. The first method can be done with batch processing; the latter cannot.

Saturation

Desaturation sucks the color out of color photographs. Complete desaturation turns a color photograph to black and white. On the other hand, sometimes a color photograph looks dull. You may be able to liven it up by increasing its saturation, that is, by making the colors seem brighter and more intense.

It's better, of course, to take photographs that don't need saturation adjustments. With experimentation in your studio, you can take fully saturated photographs that require no adjustment.

Resizing

All photographs from digital cameras need downsizing for use on the Web. You don't want to cause excessive download times for buyers to see your product photographs. You need to set up this resizing chore so that you can resize with batch processing. There's no way to get around this post-processing, so think through a process that enables you to resize quickly and systematically.

Sharpening

Almost any digital photograph will look sharper with post-processing sharpening. Does that mean you should sharpen? Again, if your photographs need sharpening, you can apply batch sharpening effectively. But the goal is to take photographs that need no sharpening, even though they might look just a little better with sharpening.

In-Camera Setting

Many digital cameras will enable you to adjust the sharpness before you even take a photograph. Choosing the appropriate setting for sharpening in your camera setup menu may help you avoid sharpening in post-processing.

Sharpening is the last step in post-processing. If you don't need to sharpen, then resizing is the last step in post processing.

One-Click

Some software offers one-button (one-click) post-processing. That is, you click on one button, and the software makes all the necessary adjustments automatically (except cropping and resizing). Photoshop Elements 3.0 has this capability and calls it the Smart Fix function. It works well. You might consider using it as your primary means of post-processing.

Software Illustrations

The software we are going to use for the illustrations in this book is Adobe Photoshop Elements 3.0 (*http://www.adobe.com*). Why? Perhaps the primary reason is that it has almost all the same features as Adobe Photoshop CS itself, which costs eight times more. Therefore, if you learn to do something that's not in this book, you will have software that will accommodate you well. At a price of $80, this software is a real bargain.

This does not mean it's the only competent software that can do the job for you. Adobe has capable competitors, such as Corel's PaintShop Pro (*http://www.corel.com*), in about the same price range. In addition, there are dozens of less expensive and less capable image editors that can do the things that we have set forth as required. There are even free image editors that can meet the requirements that we have set. For example, IrfanView (*http://irfanview.com*) is a capable free image editor that can do almost everything that you need it to do.

Image editors typically come bundled for free with the following equipment:

1. New computer
2. New video card (the board inside a PC that powers your color monitor, also known as a color card or graphics accelerator)
3. New digital camera
4. New scanner

As a result, you might already have an image editor somewhere on your hard disk that you may not be aware of. Search your hard disk looking for a program that includes a word such as *image*, *photo*, *paint*, or *editor* in the title. It may be the image editor that you need. If you purchase a new digital camera, you will have an image editor that comes with the camera.

Remember that image editors tend to be heavy-duty programs that soak up a lot of computer processing and speed. If you have a slow computer, you may want to think about upgrading (see Chapter 2).

Archive Viewers

An archive viewing program is simply one that displays your digital photographs in a matrix with thumbnails (very small images) representing the larger photograph files. These types of programs are essential to keeping organized and are very handy when it comes to processing large numbers of photographs.

Keep in mind that a lot of image editors also include a way to view your photograph archives. In other words, they will display multiple thumbnails on the screen for you. If you have an image editor that includes an archive viewer, why do you need something else?

The answer is simply that you may not. The archive viewer in your image editor, such as the one in Photoshop Elements 3.0, may be perfectly adequate. However, we say this with a caveat: Standalone archive viewers are designed to be very fast, and they enable you to look at photographs very quickly. Using your image editor to look at your photograph archives may be a slower process.

We recommend that you pick your image editor first. If it has an archive viewer that works quickly and satisfies your work style, stick with it. If it doesn't include an archive viewer, or it includes an archive viewer that is inconvenient or slow to use, then we recommend that you consider buying a separate standalone archive viewer, such as ACDSee Image Management Software (*http://www.acdsystems.com*), that will enable you to work more efficiently.

In addition, standalone archive viewers often do a lot of clever things that will help you work efficiently that archive viewers inside image editors don't necessarily do. Some of these features can be very powerful and desirable.

Two Better Than One?

The *best of breed* strategy dictates that you always use the best program of its kind. That is, you use the best image editor and the best archive viewer, which are unlikely to come in the same software package. This gives you two advantages. First, you always use the best program available for the task. Second, if you switch to a new image editor, you don't have to switch to a new archive viewer.

We recommend this strategy. Consequently, once you feel comfortable with an image editor that includes an archive editor, you might start looking around to see if you can find a better standalone archive viewer that offers more convenient features.

Summary

You need software for post-processing your photographs. If you find a capable program like Photoshop Elements 3.0, you will have an image editor and archive viewer in one software package. Otherwise, you will need an image editor and a separate archive viewer. Down the road, having a standalone archive viewer may be preferable.

II

Photography Basics

4

Traditional Photography

This chapter is an introduction to using a traditional camera with film. Because digital cameras work much the same as film cameras, this chapter is appropriate for those who know little or nothing about photography. For those who are familiar with taking photographs with cameras that have manual controls, this chapter may be of little interest to you (or it might be a good review).

The key to understanding photography is understanding how much light is absorbed (recorded) in your photograph. The camera and the film are the mechanisms that control this. With digital cameras it is the camera and the photo sensor (rather than the film) that control this.

How does the camera control the light? Two ways. First, it controls the light by changing the size of the opening (diaphragm) in the lens for the light to pass through to the film or photo sensor. Second, it controls the amount of time the shutter is open to let the light through. The shutter is normally closed, letting no light through. When you push the shutter release on the camera, the shutter opens for a certain amount of time to let the light through and then closes.

ISO

To begin, the sensitivity of the receptor determines the amount of light recorded in the photograph. The receptors are either the film in a traditional camera or the photo sensor (a digital chip) in a digital camera.

With a film camera, you change the sensitivity of your photography by using rolls of film of different sensitivities. The sensitivity is indicated by the ISO number. (A long time ago this was called the ASA number.) For instance, ISO 50 film is not very sensitive to light. Therefore, you can go out on a sunny day, where there's plenty of light, and take great pictures with ISO 50 film. If you use ISO 400 film (much more sensitive), the sunlight will tend to be too much on a sunny day. You will want to use ISO 400 film in places where it is dark or dreary. In places where it is especially dark, you might even use ISO 800 film.

Thus, one way to control the light in a photograph taken with a film camera is to change the sensitivity (ISO) of the film. Of course, this is not very convenient. If you shoot a half of roll of ISO 50 film on a sunny day, and then find yourself in a dark place where you want to take additional photographs, you might have to replace the roll of ISO 50 film with a roll of ISO 400 film in order to take decent photographs.

For a digital camera, it's a little different. The sensor itself can change its ISO sensitivity. Consequently, you can set the camera to ISO 50, or you can set it to ISO 400. Different digital cameras have different ranges of sensitivity for their sensors. In fact, digital cameras set the ISO automatically (by default) so you don't even have to worry about it. If you have your choice when you buy a camera, however, you will want to get all of the manual controls you can, and ISO is one of the adjustments you will find convenient to control from time to time.

Typical ISOs

50

100

200

400

800

1600

Notice that each sensitivity is twice as sensitive as the next lower sensitivity and half as sensitive as the next higher sensitivity. For instance, ISO 400 is twice as sensitive as ISO 200 and half as sensitive as ISO 800. Each increment is the equivalent of a *stop*, which is defined below.

Shutter

In a film camera, the shutter opens and closes to control the amount of light reaching the film. The longer it is open, the more light reaches the film. In a dark dreary place, you need the shutter to stay open longer to allow more light to reach the film. On a bright and sunny day, you need the shutter to stay open for a shorter time so as not to allow too much light to reach the film.

In film cameras, the shutter is a mechanical device. A digital camera will either have a mechanical shutter or it will simulate a mechanical shutter electronically.

Typical Shutter Speeds (seconds)

1

$\frac{1}{2}$

$\frac{1}{4}$

$\frac{1}{8}$

$\frac{1}{15}$

$\frac{1}{30}$

$\frac{1}{60}$

$\frac{1}{125}$

$\frac{1}{250}$

$\frac{1}{500}$

$\frac{1}{1000}$

Notice that each speed is twice as fast as the next slower speed and half as fast as the next higher speed. For instance, $\frac{1}{500}$ of a second is twice as fast as $\frac{1}{250}$ of a second but half as fast as $\frac{1}{1000}$ of a second. Each increment is called a *stop*.

Aperture

The diaphragm on the lens is the mechanism which enables the hole through which the light passes to change size. The hole is called the *aperture*. When the diaphragm is completely opened, the aperture is large, and it lets a huge amount of light thorough. When the diaphragm is closed to the size of a pinhole, the aperture is tiny, and it lets only a little bit of light through. With this in mind, you want to close the aperture on a bright and sunny day so as to not let too much light come through to the film or photo sensor. On a dark or dreary day you want to open the aperture so as to let as much light through as possible in order to get a good photograph.

Aperture settings, called *f-stops*, are determined by the manufacturer according to the focal length of the lens. Here are some typical f-stops for a digital camera:

Typical f-Stops

f2.8

f3.5

f5.6

f8

f11

Note that each f-stop lets in half as much light as the next lower f-stop and twice as much light as the next higher f-stop. For example, f3.5 lets in twice as much light as f5.6 but only half as much light as f2.8. Each increment is called a *stop*.

Coordination

When you take a photograph, you have to coordinate these three variables in order to take a properly exposed photograph. For a film camera, when you put in a roll of film, you set the ISO. You can't reset ISO until you take the roll of film out and put in another roll with a different ISO.

When you set the shutter speed, you do it according to a chart supplied by the film maker for a specific film (with a specific ISO). Likewise when you set the aperture, you set it according to a chart supplied by the film maker. Different types of films (with different ISOs) have different charts. The goal is to coordinate the shutter speed with the aperture so that they let in exactly the right amount of light to take a properly exposed photograph for the ISO film you have in the camera.

If you want a high-speed picture (i.e., one taken with a very fast shutter speed) in order to stop athletic or other action outdoors, you normally will coordinate that with a larger aperture (e.g., f2.8). Even though the shutter doesn't let in much light, the large aperture allows enough light to get to the film.

On the other hand, if you don't care about stopping action, such as when taking a landscape photograph, you might seek to get the greatest depth of field for your photograph. The greater the depth of field in your photograph, the more things in both the foreground and the background will be in focus. To get the greatest depth of field, the aperture needs to be the smallest (e.g., f11), not letting very much light through. In order to get a well-exposed photograph, you'll have to compensate by setting the shutter slower.

So you can see, for a film camera you essentially have two controls that you need to coordinate. The shutter speed and the aperture are settings you must make for every photograph. You set the ISO when you load a film with a specific ISO.

For a digital camera, you have three variables that you must adjust. Remember, the photo sensor's ISO (sensitivity) can be adjusted electronically by the camera. Hence, you can actually set a different ISO for each photograph. As a result, to get good photographs from a digital camera requires that you make three settings for each photograph that you take.

Automation

If you're a professional photographer, you will want the most control you can get over the camera, and you're likely to use manual controls. However, if you're an amateur photographer or even an amateur photographer with professional skills, you may be perfectly happy if you let the camera make all the adjustments for you. Indeed most cameras—even professional ones—will automatically set the shutter speed and the aperture for you for each photograph that you take. A digital camera will even adjust the ISO automatically for you for each photograph. With modern electronic technology, such automation works amazingly well for all photographers. However, there are always those times when the lighting is so crazy that you have to take manual control of the camera in order to get a good photograph.

How does the camera control the shutter speed and the aperture? It uses a light meter to determine what the lighting conditions are in the photograph that you are about to take. It uses that information to set the camera adjustments so that the camera takes a perfect picture.

In the old days, the camera's light meter indicated to you, the photographer, what manual settings to make. Cameras then evolved to the point where the camera now makes those settings for you so you don't have to do it yourself. However, for those shots where you need to control the camera yourself, the camera offers you several choices.

Aperture Priority

You can set the camera so that you control the aperture; this is called *aperture priority*. When you manually set the aperture properly, the camera will automatically take care of the other adjustments. Again, one situation in which you would want to use aperture priority would be to shoot a landscape photograph where you are concerned with having the greatest depth of field possible in order to bring everything in the foreground and the background sharply in focus. By setting the aperture small (e.g., f11), you create a photograph with this effect.

On the other hand you might want to take a picture where there's a very narrow depth of field. A portrait is a good example. In a portrait, you want to have only the person's face in focus. The person's face is the foreground. You want to have the background out of focus. If the background is in focus too, it detracts from the portrait. Therefore, for portraits you want to set the aperture large (e.g., f2.8). Aperture priority enables you to control the size of the aperture.

Shutter Priority

When you set the camera on *shutter priority*, you must set the shutter speed. According to the shutter speed you set, the camera automatically adjusts the other controls to take a well-exposed photograph. Again, you might use shutter priority to take action pictures. For instance, suppose you want to freeze the action in a local football game. Set the camera on a fast shutter speed (e.g., $\frac{1}{1000}$), stop the action, and get a very sharp photograph. The camera takes care of the other adjustments, and the camera will make the aperture larger to compensate for your fast shutter speed. For a digital camera, the camera may even adjust the ISO setting.

ISO

Automatic is the default setting in a digital camera for the ISO. That means the digital camera will set the ISO automatically for each photograph you take. The question becomes, Why do I want to set the ISO? The answer to that varies with different digital cameras. For inexpensive digital cameras with small sensors, you get the best photographs at low ISOs. Most cameras with small photo sensors will start to show degraded (*noisy*) photographs at ISOs over 100 or 200. Virtually all will show noise at ISOs of 400 and above. On the other hand, expensive SLR cameras with large sensors can take high-quality photographs at ISOs of 400, 800, and even 1600.

Noise

Noise is individual pixels showing incorrect colors. It shows most distinctly in broad expanses of identical (or similar) color in photographs. For instance, a large dark grey shadow in a digital photograph may slow tiny flecks of a slightly lighter color.

Thus, if you have an expensive camera with a large photo sensor, you probably won't worry too much about ISO settings. But if you're using an inexpensive camera with a small sensor, you might want to set the ISO at 50 or 100 permanently in order to take the highest quality photographs you can get. In that case, the camera doesn't have any choice. When you set the ISO manually, the camera will not adjust it.

Manual Adjustments

You need to learn to do manual adjustments, even if you don't use them. Learning helps you understand what's going on in the process of taking a photograph. You normally change the ISO, the shutter speed, or the aperture by standard increments (stops). One stop is twice as much as the prior increment and half as much as the next increment. So if you increase the ISO from 50 to 100, you increase it one stop. Notice that the ISO doubled from 50 to 100. To increase the ISO another stop, you have to change it to 200. If you change it another stop beyond that, you have to change it to 400. So going up each stop is twice as much as the setting before, and going down each stop is half as much as the setting before.

For the shutter speed, you might start with $1/4$ of a second. In order to go up a stop, you have to go to $1/8$ of a second. Next is $1/16$ and so forth.

The aperture is a more complex measurement, and the manufacturer of the lens normally determines the stops and labels them for each particular lens. Therefore, you simply read the settings for the lens. They are one stop apart.

How Do All of These Work Together?

The chart below shows the stops for a lens together with shutter speeds and apertures. At the top of the chart are the settings to keep the most light out, and at the bottom of the chart are the settings to let the most light in—all in one-stop increments:

ISO	Shutter Speed	Aperture
50	$^1/_{1000}$	f 11
100	$^1/_{500}$	f 8
200	$^1/_{250}$	f 5.6
400	$^1/_{125}$	f 3.5
800	$^1/_{60}$	f 2.8
1600	$^1/_{30}$	
	$^1/_{15}$	
	$^1/_{8}$	
	$^1/_{4}$	
	$^1/_{2}$	

With film cameras, you only have two adjustments to make: the shutter speed and the aperture. That makes manually adjusting the camera relatively simple. With the advent of digital cameras, however, you can now adjust the ISO setting too. With three variables, making the adjustments manually can be mind-boggling.

That's why many professionals allow the camera to make at least one or two of the adjustments automatically for each photograph. You need to understand how this works. Why? Because you may have a reason for making a specific setting.

For instance, if you want to get the highest quality photograph with an inexpensive digital camera (with a small sensor), you may want to set the ISO at 100. Likewise, if you want to stop some fast moving action, like the players in a football game, you may want to set the shutter to a high speed, say $^1/_{1000}$ of a second. Similarly, if you're taking a photograph for which you specifically need a greater depth of field (e.g., landscape), you will need to set the aperture to a high f-stop.

Whenever you have the desire to set one or two of these three, the other one or two must be adjusted also. In most cases, it's probably best to let the camera make the adjustments automatically. Nonetheless, as we mentioned before, there are certain situations where you may want to set all three yourself. And to make such settings work well, you have to understand how these three adjustments work together.

Examples

Set your point-and-shoot digital camera at ISO 100 for all your work. This is a good strategy. At 100 you have twice as much sensitivity as at 50, but you're unlikely to get noise. Now, suppose you set the camera to automatic, and it shows that it's going to take the next photograph at f3.5 at $1/125$ of a second. You would like to have greater depth of field for your product photography just to make sure each entire product is in focus. You decide to set the f-stop at f8. What is the appropriate shutter setting? Well, you've shut down the f-stop to f8, so you now need to slow down the shutter speed two stops to compensate. You must set the new shutter speed at $1/30$ of a second.

Normally, for hand-held photography, $1/30$ of a second would be too slow. Hand-held photography should seldom be slower than $1/125$ of a second, and $1/250$ is better. But you normally shoot products in a studio with a tripod, so $1/30$ is OK.

Conclusion

A good way to get a feel for these adjustments is to look at the charts published by film manufacturers for a specific film (i.e., a specific ISO) that show the relationship between shutter speed and aperture for various lighting conditions. For instance, you can find charts for Kodak film at the Kodak website (*http://www.kodak.com*). In those charts you will see how these adjustments change for different lighting conditions such as sunny and clear; hazy; dark overcast; twilight; low light; and so forth. If you can understand these three adjustments, you have made a giant step forward in understanding how to take excellent photographs.

5

Digital Photography

Digital cameras work pretty much the same way as film cameras. All the same principles apply. There are a few extra things, however, to keep in mind when using a digital camera. We have already covered setting the ISO in Chapter 4, but there's more. Most of these extras are not something to worry about, but you should understand them nonetheless so as to be aware of the additional factors in taking high-quality digital photographs.

Camera Features

Digital cameras have a lot of features that traditional cameras do not. The list here is a short list relevant to eBay product photography and is not meant to be a comprehensive list for more general use.

Image Size

A digital camera can take images of differing size quality. Therefore, you must set the size and quality you want to take. This is an easy determination to make. You need to set your camera to take pictures at the largest size possible and the highest quality possible while keeping in mind the number of photographs you can store conveniently on a memory card. The chart below indicates the choices you might have for a typical 3-MP digital camera.

Resolution (pixels)	Quality	Images (16 MB Card)
2048 × 1536	Super-Fine	8
	Fine	16
	Normal	32
1600 × 1200	Super-Fine	14
	Fine	26
	Normal	52
1024 × 768	Super-Fine	25
	Fine	46
	Normal	84
640 × 480	Super-Fine	58
	Fine	94
	Normal	165

The larger resolution dimensions (pixels) are higher quality because they pack more pixels into the same photograph than do lower resolutions.

The quality designation (different words for different manufacturers) indicate the amount of JPEG compression applied to the photographs as they are saved to the camera's memory chip. JPEG compression is lossy; that is, it loses quality. The loss of quality depends on the amount of compression. For the camera above, Super-Fine is the highest quality with the least JPEG compression. Normal is the lowest quality with the most compression.

For the camera above, 2048 × 1536 pixels at Super-Fine gives you the highest quality picture possible with which to work and create a good eBay item photograph. Naturally, the more megapixels you have, the higher resolution your photographs can be. The chart below indicates the largest image you can get from cameras with various megapixel ratings.

Resolution (pixels)	MP
2048 × 1536	3
2272 × 1704	4
2560 × 1920	5
2848 × 2136	6
3072 × 2304	7
3264 × 2448	8

As we've said before, we don't believe you need more than a 3-MP camera to do high-quality eBay photography. Since you get an image that's about 2000 × 1500 pixels with a 3-MP camera, that appears to be substantial overkill to create a photograph that's 400 × 300 pixels for your eBay auction ad. Indeed, it's about 25 times as big as you need. (This assumes that you fill the frame with the item being photographed, a technique we recommend you use.)

With this information in mind, our recommendation to you is that you set your digital camera at its highest resolution and image quality, use a memory card with plenty of memory, and then forget about it.

File Format

Another choice you need to make is the file format in which the camera will store your photographs. We recommend JPEG. Although TIF files and RAW files (used in more expensive cameras) are higher quality with less compression, JPEG files are more than enough to accommodate your purposes in taking eBay product photographs. If you use TIF files or RAW files, they will require extra time in your post-processing for very little additional quality, if any, for online display. Therefore, we believe you're wasting your time to use these more robust file formats. Stick with JPEG.

White Balance

Different light sources have different color temperatures. The kind of light you get on a bright, clear day is a very high color temperature. The kind of light you get in a room with an incandescent light is a lower color temperature. If you avoid mixing different kinds of light together in one photograph, it may make your photography easier.

Since we cover white balance in Chapter 6, we won't dwell on it here. Nonetheless, we should mention that white balance is handled in film cameras by using different types of film. There is indoor film that is white balanced for tungsten light, and there is outdoor film that is white balanced for sunny days. For digital cameras, the white balance is a setting. Like many other electronic settings, the camera can do it automatically, or you can do it manually. As for all camera settings, you might find yourself in situations where you need to set the white balance yourself rather than let the camera do it automatically.

Viewfinder

Unless you have a digital SLR camera which shows the exact photograph to be taken through the viewfinder, you are not always going to see the picture you take through your viewfinder. Optical viewfinders (not through the lens) have a parallax distortion, particularly close up. The closer you get to the subject of the photograph, the greater the parallax error. The greater the parallax error, the less likely it is that you will be able to tell exactly what's going to be in the photograph and what's not.

Fortunately, where digital cameras are superior to film cameras in this regard is that digital cameras have an LCD screen on the back, which shows exactly the photograph that you are going to take. In addition, some digital cameras do not have an optical viewfinder but rather a digital viewfinder. A digital viewfinder is like the LCD screen and provides an accurate view of the photograph to be taken. The problem with digital viewfinders is that many of them are low resolution. Low resolution digital viewfinders sometimes make it difficult to take photographs.

Under the circumstances, it would seem that a digital SLR would be ideal for shooting eBay photographs. But a digital SLR, a relatively expensive camera, is not necessary. As mentioned above, when shooting close-up photographs of items, you are more likely to rely on the LCD screen on the back of the camera than you are on the viewfinder itself. When shooting large objects outside such as cars, almost any viewfinder will work well.

Macro Photography

A great advantage of most digital cameras is that they take good macro photographs without any additional equipment. Macro photography is simply taking photographs of small things and very small things (e.g., jewelry). Because they have smaller lenses, most inexpensive digital cameras have good macro capability. You have to turn on the camera's macro mode.

The alternative for more expensive digital cameras with larger lenses and for digital SLR cameras is not so desirable. First, you may have to add a close-up lens on the front of your lens. This is inconvenient. When you're doing normal photography, you'll have to remove the close-up lens. Your best bet if you're going to use a digital SLR to do macro photography is to buy a macro lens for it. Such lenses tend to be expensive and are an additional expense for your eBay photography.

Of course if you are not going to do any macrophotography, this discussion is not relevant. But if you are doing general photography, where you shoot large things one day and small things another, you'll need to have macro capability.

Image Review

One of the great advantages of a digital camera is that you can use the LCD screen on the back of the camera to not only see the photograph you are about to take but also to review the photographs that you've taken. You don't have to wait for the film to be developed and the prints to be made before you can make sure that you've taken a photograph adequate for your purposes. This is not a perfect review procedure that works 100 percent of the time—primarily because the LCD image is small—but nonetheless it works pretty well. This capability is one of the better features of digital cameras, particularly for eBay product photography.

Preview

The capability to preview the shot you will take is a convenient feature. You should be able to see exactly what you're going to get on the LCD screen. This is one reason why photo lights are better than flashes for simple product photography. For a flash photograph,

you have to wait until after you take the shot to evaluate the quality
of the resulting photograph.

ISO Setting

There's no need here to rehash our discussion of ISO discussed in
Chapter 4 except to remind you that another advantage of digital cameras is that you can set the ISO. This can be particularly important
when you take photographs in the same environment all the time,
such as in a studio where the lighting is pretty much the same for most
of your product photographs.

Other Capabilities

Because a digital image can be managed right inside the camera by the
camera itself, digital cameras have a huge advantage over film cameras. However, most of the things that digital cameras can do are
beyond the scope of this book. Consequently, there are a lot of digital
camera capabilities that we do not cover here because such capabilities
are designed for general photography, and they're not a convenience or
a significant benefit for people taking eBay product photographs.

Digital Zoom

One of the clever things a digital camera can do is zoom in to a greater
extent than can its optical zoom lens. Digitally, you can achieve a telescopic effect twice or three times more than the lens of the camera can.
Unfortunately, even though you can do it, it doesn't work very well.
When you start zooming digitally, the overall image degrades rapidly,
and pretty soon you may end up with a photograph that lacks quality
and sharpness. Therefore, we recommend that you never use the digital zoom capability of your digital camera. Just because the capability
exists does not mean that it is appropriate to use it.

Shutter Lag

You will notice that on most inexpensive digital cameras there is a lag between the time you push the shutter down and when the camera actually snaps the picture. That lag can be a second, a half second, a quarter of a second. For eBay photography, it's something you probably will not need to worry about because your subject (i.e., the eBay item) presumably is always steady. That is, it doesn't move. So a shutter lag shouldn't make any difference for most eBay photography. Where a shutter lag might interfere with your photography is when taking action photographs.

Similar to shutter lag but not identical is the fact that most digital cameras require a start-up time. It might be several seconds or longer from the time you turn on the camera until you can start to use it to take photographs. Again, for product photography this is not a big deal. For action photography where you might need to turn on your camera and take photographs immediately on the spur of the moment, a quick start-up time would be important to you.

Summary

Again, let us simply state that a digital camera is not much different from a film camera in the way that it handles light. You are going to have to be concerned with f-stops and shutter speeds. You can probably set the ISO and the white balance and forget them, particularly for studio photography where the light environment is a constant. This chapter outlines some of the features that make a digital camera different from a film camera, and most of them are desirable features. What these features mean to you is that you can take better photographs with a digital camera for displaying your eBay items online than you ever could with a film camera.

III

Product Photography Indoors

6

Indoor Photography Basics

The key to indoor photography is—guess what?—light. If you can control the light, you can easily take great product photographs for your eBay auction ads. If you can't, your photographs may be substandard and even exhibit strange effects, such as weird and unattractive color tints. Fortunately, indoor light is not like outdoor light. Outdoors you have to take what you get, and that may change from hour to hour or even from minute to minute. Indoors, you can have total control over light. It's just a matter of knowing what to do with basic lighting equipment to make light work for you.

Light

In order to control light, we need a means of evaluating it as well as a means of measuring it. The built-in light meter in your camera measures the light intensity in order to set a proper exposure for taking a photograph. We use light temperature measured in degrees Kelvin to evaluate light. Whatever the light source, you want your camera to show the light source as being white. But not all light is the same color. Here are some examples:

Blue sky	11000K
Hazy sky	8000K
Daylight at noon	5500K
Typical daylight	5000K
Studio flood lights	3000K
Household light bulbs	2500K

Note that color temperature is not the same as brightness. Rather, it's the relative intensity of blue to red. Thus, household lights give you a yellowish light while a sunless blue sky gives you a bluish light.

The process of setting a digital camera to show light from the light source as being white light is called setting the white balance. (In a film camera, the same is accomplished by using different types of film.) Digital cameras are pretty good at setting the white balance automatically, so why bother to comment on white balance?

Indoor light comes from different sources (e.g., daylight from a window and incandescent light from a light bulb), and that can result in some atypical effects in your photographs. Consequently, the easiest way to control light and white balance may be to use a uniform source of light. However, digital cameras do a good job of handling a mixed-light environment with the white balance set on automatic, and uniform light is not an absolute necessity for good product photography.

Incandescent Lights

Incandescent lights come in different color temperatures. As you can see from the list above, household light bulbs (tungsten) are about 2,500K. Studio lights are typically from 3000K to 3400K. To get the color temperature up, incandescent lights burn hot, and you usually need considerable wattage to provide adequate brightness. This is the traditional source of indoor light for photography.

Quartz-Halogen Lights

You can treat quartz-halogen lights as identical to tungsten lights. Their design enables smaller bulbs, but they otherwise work the same.

Fluorescent Lights

If you mix normal fluorescent lights and incandescent lights, you may get a color cast to your photographs. Therefore, don't mix where you can avoid doing so. But what about fluorescent lights alone? Normal fluorescent lights are cooler or bluer than incandescent lights (i.e., a higher color temperature), typically 4100K to 6700K. You can use them most effectively if you use them to the exclusion of another light source of a different color temperature. Unfortunately, manufacturers of household fluorescent lighting usually don't print the color temperature on the tubes, and overhead fluorescent tubes aren't as bright as you might need for all your eBay photography. When using them, you will have to set the camera shutter speed low and make careful use of a tripod.

One way to get around this is to use fluorescent spirals (simulating household light bulbs) inside a metal photo reflector. The problem in doing so is that the overhead fluorescent tubes and the fluorescent spirals inside the reflector may be different color temperatures.

A better practice is to use special fluorescent tubes and spirals with the same color temperatures. You can get these from photography supply catalogs, other professional lighting sources, and wholesale sources.

They cost more, but the color temperature is printed on the tube or spiral (or on the container). You are assured that you have the information to make a match. Moreover, they are usually manufactured for photographic work at the color temperature of daylight, 5000K to 5400K, making them compatible with the daylight coming into a room. A daylight color temperature also has the advantage of seeming natural.

Warm Fluorescents

You can buy warm fluorescent tubes with a color temperature that matches incandescent photo lights from commercial lighting sources. Keep this in mind if you use incandescent studio lights.

Although there's more to fluorescent lights than just the color temperature, knowing the color temperature is a good place to start when evaluating them for use as a photographic light source or as a general light source in your studio.

Natural Light

Daylight usually comes indoors through a window, skylight, or door. You will want to control the light from such sources during the times that you shoot your product photographs. If you use fluorescent lights with a color temperature of 5000K to 5400K, however, daylight will be completely compatible with your indoor photography.

If you use natural light indoors with no other light source, it can work well as an indoor lighting source in certain situations. For instance, natural light can be useful for photographing large items in place such as sofas.

Flash

Casual flash photography does not work well for product photography. Too much glare reflects from the item photographed. Nonetheless, many professionals use a flash for their product photography. Unfortunately, professional flash photography requires expensive equipment and is quite complex. Therefore, it is not suitable for most eBay businesspeople and is beyond the scope of this book.

There are some situations where you may want to try a fill-in flash, if available in your camera, to reduce shadows. But otherwise we don't recommend flash photography.

Diffused Light

Using sources of uniform light isn't the sole objective. For product photography, the light source most often should be diffused. Otherwise, your photographs will show too much glare in many cases.

Reflections

Without diffusion, the light source will cause hot spots (white spots) in the photograph. The area around the white spots will have washed out details that interfere with a viewer's perception of the product. In short, the photograph will not be as attractive and may not effectively show enough detail to prospective buyers for them to make a purchasing decision.

Spectral Highlights

The technical name for glare or white spots is *spectral highlights*. Accordingly, we will refer to glare as spectral highlights in the remainder of the book.

In contrast, diffused light does not cause overwhelming glare (intense spectral highlights) but rather brings out the details in a product as well as makes a more attractive photograph. Therefore, one of the primary lessons of this book is to use diffused light to shoot your product photographs in most cases.

Beware of Mirrors

Think of every side (every surface) of a product as a mirror. Granted, most products do not make good mirrors, but they reflect light nonetheless. Even products that are flat black can show intense spectral highlights from an intense undiffused light source. So, again, think of every surface of a product as a mirror. It's your job to keep those mirrors from showing intense spectral highlights. You can only do so by using diffused light.

Diffusion

When is light diffused? When it doesn't create intense spectral highlights. Let's look at some examples. First, when the light source is larger than the item and very close to it, there are no intense spectral highlights. The light is uniform across the item. The camera will adjust the exposure to take a good photograph (see Figure 6.1).

Figure 6.1 When the light source is larger than the item and close to it, the light is even.

Second, when the light source is far away from the item, the light is diffused simply by the distance. The item will show spectral highlights, but the spectral highlights will be tiny. With a light source far away, however, you may not have enough light to take a good photograph easily and efficiently (see Figure 6.2).

Figure 6.2 When the light source is far away from the item, the light is diffused by distance.

Third, when a light source is smaller than the product or not close to it, yet not a long way from it, intense spectral highlights become a problem. And guess what? This is the typical studio shooting situation (see Figure 6.3).

Figure 6.3 The normal situation is one where the light source is smaller than the item or not close to it so as to cause intense spectral highlights.

A studio light source is usually far enough away from a product and relatively smaller so as to cause intense spectral highlights. Light sources are usually not so far away as to be effectively diffused because a photographer has to have enough light to see what he or she is doing and to take a photograph with a reasonably high shutter speed. Consequently, you will be continually concerned with diffusing your light sources as you shoot your product photographs in a normal studio environment. The question then arises, How do you diffuse light?

Studio Lights

Incandescent lights include all tungsten light sources from household light bulbs to studio flood lights. These lights have a tungsten filament that burns bright. Even when the bulb containing the filament is coated inside with a diffusing substance, it still burns so bright it requires additional diffusion. Quartz halogen bulbs are similar.

Fluorescent spirals have a glowing gas instead of a tungsten filament and appear to be a little more diffused than incandescent bulbs. Still, they need to be diffused to avoid intense spectral highlights.

In addition, to maximize the effectiveness of any light source, you need to concentrate it. The primary way to do this is to put the light source inside a metal reflector, that is, a floodlight reflector (see Figure 6.4). This makes the light source even more intense and larger. Thus, the need for diffusion becomes even greater.

Floodlight Reflectors and Stands

Not only does a floodlight reflector concentrate the light by a means that can be directed (aimed) at the product, but it also keeps the light out of the eyes of the photographer.

In addition, lights and floodlight reflectors are normally used on a light stand so that you can easily move them around to get the best possible lighting for a product.

Figure 6.4 A typical floodlight reflector (and light source) on a light stand. ©2004 Smith-Victor Corporation. All rights reserved.

The best ways to diffuse light sources are with frontal diffusers, soft boxes, and umbrellas. Frontal diffusers attach to the floodlight reflector (on the front) and diffuse the light as it emits from the light source (see Figure 6.5). These diffusers are translucent and made of glass or fireproof plastic attached so as to allow heat to escape from inside the reflector. The reflector is aimed at the product. Diffusers are usually detachable so as to permit you maximum flexibility in using your light source. This is an inexpensive means of diffusion but not always the most effective.

Figure 6.5 Frontal diffuser for floodlight reflector. ©2004 Smith-Victor Corporation. All rights reserved.

Perhaps a more effective means of diffusion for many situations is the soft box. This is essentially a big box with the light source inside. The front of the box has a translucent screen through which the light passes to the product (see Figure 6.6). The screen diffuses the light. The front of the box is aimed at the product. Soft boxes are usually large and relatively expensive.

Figure 6.6 Soft box. ©2004 Smith-Victor Corporation. All rights reserved.

An even more effective means of diffusion is an umbrella. The light source is directed (aimed) at the inside of an open umbrella. The umbrella reflects the light back. The reflected light is highly diffused. The entire apparatus (the light stand with the umbrella) is aimed at the product (see Figure 6.7).

Figure 6.7 Umbrella diffusers (without lights). ©2004 Smith-Victor Corporation. All rights reserved.

The inside of the umbrella can be a reflective color or have a reflective coating. Umbrellas and umbrella clamps for light stands are inexpensive.

Safety

Incandescent lights burn very hot. Do not use makeshift diffusers that place combustable materials such as plastic near incandescent bulbs. Always use professional photographic equipment. You don't want your studio to burn down when you go into another room to answer the telephone. Frontal diffusers, umbrellas, and light stands are reasonably priced.

Tents

You erect a tent on a table top. You use your lights outside the tent without any diffusion. The tent provides the diffusion. You place a product inside the tent, and you shoot your product photographs. Works great. You can buy such a tent for as little as $50. Typically tents are limited to tabletop-sized items or smaller. But that doesn't have to be the case. You can buy and use larger tents too.

Light Boxes

Light boxes are boxes with lights inside. The lights are typically behind several full-length, full-width translucent panels, which effectively diffuse the light. Your product goes inside the box to be photographed.

These work great for jewelry and other small items, although there are light boxes large enough to accommodate tabletop-sized items too. Light boxes are expensive, but if you take a large volume of photographs, the extra expense can be cost-effective.

Natural Light

Natural light is naturally diffused unless it is direct sunlight streaming through a window, skylight, or door. You will have to use something (even a bed sheet) to diffuse direct sunlight or wait until a different time of the day. Without direct sunlight, however, you won't necessarily have a diffusion problem, although you may have to establish a second source of lighting (i.e. use a reflector) to take a good photograph. The problem with natural light, of course, is that you don't have much control over it.

Flash

You can tape a piece of translucent white plastic (e.g., garbage bag) over the flash window on your digital camera to diffuse the light. In the alternative, you can buy a plastic diffuser for a flash attachment. Neither of these diffusion techniques works well, but they're better than nothing. Another well-known technique is to use a flash attachment and bounce the flash off the ceiling or off a wall for diffusion. However, since we do not recommend using a flash in the first place, we will not cover flash diffusion techniques.

Placement

How many lights do you need, and where do you place them? Well common wisdom among professional photographers indicates that you need three lights. You position the first two in front of the subject to be photographed, one offset from the centerline 45 degrees to the left and the other offset from the centerline 45 degrees to the right. You use the third light to backlight the subject. This is the general rule (see Figure 6.8).

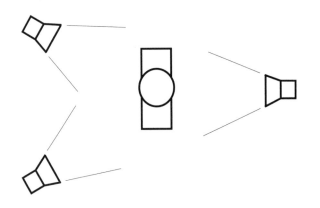

Figure 6.8   General lighting setup for studio photography. But you do not need the backlight for product photography.

Not all professional photographers shoot products, however. Most photograph people. So for product photography, the one part of the general rule you can forget is the backlight. That leaves you with two lights placed as shown above, and that's a reasonable general guideline with which to approach the photography of products.

Vertical Placement

If you can place a light high enough so that it points down to the subject being photographed at a 45 degree angle, that can be a good placement for product photography, particularly if you wish to show natural shadows.

Surfaces, Mirrors

To set up your lighting, however, you must keep in mind the goal of using diffused light: Avoid intense specular highlights and show the detail of the products you photograph. As we mentioned above in the section on diffused light, every surface of a product acts as a mirror. Your job is to avoid intense specular highlights from those surfaces. Accordingly, the first reality of product photography is that: The general rule of lighting placement is only a starting point. Indeed, practical lighting for product photography requires experimentation.

Keep Notes

If you need to move lights around to get the proper placement for each product you shoot and if you need to shoot a lot of different products, you might find that you can't work efficiently. There are three ways to work more efficiently, however, and you will save yourself a lot of time to keep them in mind.

First, keep notes on your setups for different products. For instance, you might have categories such as jewelry, small items, tabletop items, glassware, and so forth. Your notes should tell you what lights to use and where to place them. Why reinvent the wheel? Keep track of what you've learned already through your experimentation.

Second, take a photograph of your setup for each type of product. Keep the photograph with the corresponding notes.

Third, use reflectors. Reflectors are, in effect, additional lights, albeit weak ones. You can move reflectors around much more efficiently than moving lights, as we will discuss in the next section.

Reflectors

You need reflectors to supplement the electric light sources that you use in the studio. You can buy reflectors of various sizes that are inexpensive. They typically consist of steel loops with a reflective fabric stretched across, and you can twist them to collapse them for storage and transportation (see Figure 6.9).

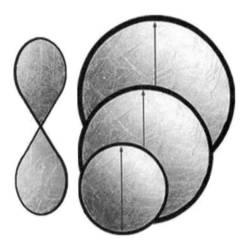

Figure 6.9 Professional reflectors (photo from Adorama).

A stand is required to use collapsible reflectors effectively, however, which can become awkwardly inconvenient in your studio—in a word, inefficient. So is there a better way?

In fact, we don't recommend professional collapsible reflectors for several reasons. They are not always handy to use. The stands are just extra equipment to get in the way. And there is a less expensive and more handy alternative.

The Handy Way

We recommend that you buy sheets of white foam-board at an art supply store. This is a stiff durable board with white paper on each side. Buy the largest board you can get in your car or truck, take it home, and cut it into various size rectangular pieces to use as reflectors. For instance, you might use one or two boards of 5 × 8 inches each for jewelry. For small items, you might find a couple of 10 × 15 inch boards handy. For desktop items, a couple of 30 × 36 inch boards might work. For large items in place (e.g., sofa), even a 48 × 48 inch board will work.

Reflector Props

How do you hold the boards in place? Prop them up with heavy objects like an unopened bottle of soda or large bottle of juice. If you want to add a professional ambiance to your studio, you can fill your small and large prop bottles with something heavy like sand, stones, or jelly beans and seal them. Make sure the prop bottles have broad and stable bases. For example, Gatorade bottles work well.

Propping up rectangles of foam-board with heavy bottles is much more handy in most cases than moving around professional collaps-ible reflectors on stands. And it's surely less expensive.

Portability

You can use collapsible reflectors efficiently away from your studio where it's not convenient to lug heavy bottles and large foam-board reflectors.

What's the point of the reflectors? They simply provide better and more flexible lighting. For instance, suppose you light the product from the left and right without much of an offset angle simply to keep the lights out of your way while you work. The product seems a little dark in the front. You place a foam-board reflector to catch the light from one of the light sources and shine it on the front of the product. Works like a charm. Because you always have to experiment, foam-board reflectors can make your photography much more efficient. They are very easy to move around.

Stanley's Way

Stanley's 40 years of experience taking photographs has led him to take an even more simple approach to product lighting. He uses only one diffused light overhead on a boom to light the product (see Figure 6.10). Then he uses foam-board reflectors to fill in light around the bottom of the product. He likes this approach because we are used to seeing things with light falling on them, not directed at them. This lighting scheme tends to look more natural than others. Then too, there is one less light stand to trip over or otherwise get in the way.

Figure 6.10 Overhead boom on a stand (Manfrotto 3398 – photo from Adorama).

If you can only afford to buy a minimal amount of photographic equipment, then a stand, a boom, and one diffused light together with an assortment of foam-board reflectors might be perfectly adequate for your studio.

What's the Bottom Line?

There is no bottom line. There are a variety of diffused lighting sources. There are a variety of placements. There are a variety of sizes and shapes of products. And you have plenty of flexibility in using foam-board reflectors. The name of the game is experimentation. Find out what works and remember it (i.e., keep notes).

For instance, light boxes are great for photographing jewelry, but they're not cheap. Tents are great for photographing small products, but tents get in the way if you photograph larger products too. An overhead diffused light source and some foam-board reflectors can enable you to shoot a variety of products with an inexpensive and efficient production line. There is no single correct way to set up your lighting.

Sample Lighting Assemblies

Just to give you an idea of pricing (not necessarily a recommendation), the Smith Victor KT900 lighting kit, which retails for about $275, contains the following equipment:

2 12-inch floodlight reflectors
1 5-inch floodlight reflector
3 sockets, cordsets, and stand mounts
2 white umbrellas and umbrella mounts
2 ECT 500-watt photoflood lamps
1 ECA 250-watt photoflood lamp
3 Raven RS8 8-foot aluminum stands
1 light cart with wheels
1 lighting guide

Although you may decide that this particular setup is not for you, it shows that safe, professional lighting does not have to be terribly expensive (see Figure 6.11).

If you prefer diffusers over umbrellas, you might try a Smith Victor DP12 clip-on frontal diffuser for 12-inch floodlight reflectors (about $25). See Figure 6.5 earlier in this chapter.

If you like Stanley's overhead-light approach, then you might buy one high-quality boom such as the Manfrotto 3398 boom and stand (about $115). See Figure 6.10 earlier in this chapter. You will have to add the requisite floodlight reflector, light fixture, and bulb assembly (e.g., Smith Victor A120 for about $90) plus a frontal diffuser (about $25) or an umbrella with a stand clamp (under $60).

Figure 6.11 Smith Victor KT900 lighting kit. ©2004 Smith-Victor Corporation. All rights reserved.

Background

Keep it simple. A knowledgeable art director for an advertising firm could write a whole book on backgrounds for product photography. You don't have to worry about that kind of sophistication. Use a simple white or grey background for all your product photography. How do you arrange that? Use a roll of paper.

Look for rolls of seamless background paper in photographic supply catalogs. Typical widths are 26 inches, 53 inches, and 107 inches. You can buy a stand for the paper at a reasonable price. But you might want to use a broomstick hung from the ceiling with loops of parachute cord instead to hold the roll of seamless paper.

What does *seamless* mean? First, you place the roll of paper near the ceiling with a stand or a hanging fixture. Next, you unroll the paper so that it comes down the wall and then comes forward across a table or across the floor. Instead of showing a line where two planes intersect (e.g., the wall and the floor), the curve of the paper shows no line. There is a seamless transition, in effect, between the vertical plane and the horizontal plane. This is also called an *infinite horizon*. It makes an undistracting background for product photography.

If you are shooting on a table, use clamps from a hardware store to clamp the paper to the forward edge of the table. If you are shooting on the floor, use gaffers tape to tape the paper to the floor in front of the product. Unless you leave your studio permanently set up for ongoing product photography, reroll the paper after you are finished shooting.

Usually you can set up the paper many times if you are careful. When it becomes dirty or torn, however, just cut off the unsightly portion and unroll more paper. This is an inexpensive means of creating a professional background. Don't try to cut corners by doing something else that will invariably be more trouble and look more sloppy.

You can photograph small products on a tabletop using just a sheet of drawing paper from an art store. Lay it flat in front. Clamp it to the front edge of the table. Then prop it up in back with a couple of the prop bottles that you use for foam-board reflectors. You will have a seamless background adequate for photographing small items.

Alas, some products just don't look their best with a white or grey background. You can use simple alternatives. You can buy rolls of seamless background paper in different colors—but avoid dark colors. You can use velvet, satin, silk, other fabrics, or colored poster board on which to place a small product for a more elegant presentation. For, instance, you might place a gold diamond ring on a swatch of black velvet or blue velvet. The swatch is the background for the photograph. Whatever alternative you use, make it a plain one. You don't want the background to distract a buyer from the product itself.

From Beginning to End

What about a procedure that starts with just the right amount of light, takes your shot for you, and enables you to view the results on your computer monitor? Slick! That would be Ortery's Photosimile 200 light box (*http://ortery.com*). Here's how it works (see Figure 6.12):

1. Turn on your computer and start in the Photosimile 200 (formerly the Coloreal eBox).

2. Open the Image Creator program and get the working screen. The lights will go on in the box.

3. Put your item in the box. Use props, if necessary, to set it up.

4. Click on Preview. You will see the item on your monitor.

5. Adjust the setup in the box if necessary. It may take a quick manual adjustment.

6. Click on Snap (i.e., to take a snapshot).

7. Review your photograph on your monitor. What you see is what the prospective buyers get.

8. Save it to a folder, or use Image Creator for your post-processing.

9. For post-processing in Image Creator, you can adjust brightness and contrast, saturation, and size. You can also crop and rename files. Then you can save the file(s) to a folder. This program also has batch processing capabilities.

How does all this work? Pretty well. Look at Photos 48, 61, 74, and 75 appearing at intervals in the center section.

What's this system got going for it? Well, there are a lot of pluses:

- The system is efficient, and when you're done with a photograph, you know you've got something that will be adequate.

- You don't have to experiment with lights. They're diffused and the same for each shot. For certain items, you will need to use and adjust props.

- You never have to touch the camera. It's controlled by the software.

- The system is, in effect, a complete photograph assembly line.

- The system doesn't take up much space.

- It's easy to use.

- You can shoot from the front, instead of the top, by opening the door and using a reflective screen in its place. The screen has an opening through which you can take photographs.

- It accommodates a variety of standard high-quality digital cameras. The one Joe used with it was the 4-MP Canon A80, an excellent camera.

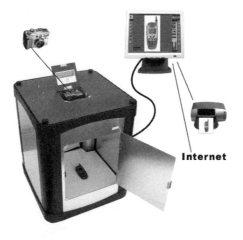

Figure 6.12 Photosimile 200 system. ©2005 Ortery Technologies, Inc.

What are the drawbacks? There are a few:

- You need to have a computer in your studio, and it needs to be a fast one to power this system. Joe used a 1.2 GHz PC, and it seemed a little slow. However, note that a computer cannot work faster than the camera that's plugged into the system.

- The system works well for opaque items without props. For other items (e.g., shiny items and jewelry), however, you will need to learn how to use the box. A few props like colored drawing paper, poster board, and cloth will help you take good photographs of shiny items. Ortery will give you some tips on using the proper setups, including such techniques as employing boxes or risers to raise the elevation of items.

- Although the box is large, many items will still be too big for it.

- The Preview image is lower quality than the final photograph.

As you can see from the Image Creator screen, the system is simple to operate (see Figure 6.13). It's all there on your monitor screen.

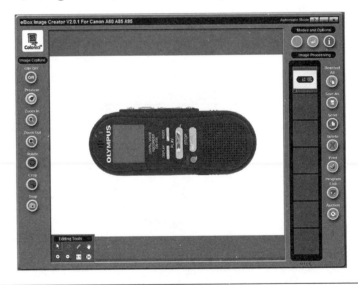

Figure 6.13 Image Creator software interface showing a photograph of an Olympus digital voice recorder.

This is not necessarily an endorsement of the Photosimile 200. It does and will have able competitors. The best advice we can give regarding these systems is to fully evaluate one before you buy it to make sure it lives up to your expectations. If it does, you'll be a step ahead of other eBay businesses in making your eBay photography as efficient as it can be. Some of these systems are reasonably priced, but they're not cheap. You need to factor the price and the savings of your time and effort that such a system facilitates in order to decide whether it's cost-effective. If you have low volume, you will probably not buy such a system.

Shooting for the Book

This chapter seems the appropriate place to mention which cameras and lights the authors used to take the product photographs you see in the center color section of this book. The other photographic equipment used is mentioned in each chapter.

Cameras

Stanley, a professional product photographer, used two excellent cameras. The first was a 6-MP Nikon D70 digital SLR camera (circa 2004) with various Nikon lenses (see review at *http://www.steves-digi-cams.com/2004_reviews/nikon_d70.html*). The second was a Fuji F-700 digital point-and-shoot camera (circa 2003) with the 3-MP sensor that has the equivalent of an additional 3 MPs, making it in effect a hybrid 6-MP camera (see review at *http://www.steves-digicams.com/2003_reviews/fuji_f700.html*). Stanley's rules for taking photographs for the the book were that he could use whatever camera he wanted to and do whatever post-processing he wanted to.

Joe, on the other hand, played the role of an eBay businessperson. He might have used his 8-MP Minolta A2 prosumer digital camera (circa 2004), but that would have been considerable overkill. He wanted to use his wife's 3-MP Canon A70 point-and-shoot camera (circa 2003), a great camera, but that turned out to be lost when it came time to take the photographs for this book. So, he borrowed a 2-MP Olympus C-2020 point-and-shoot camera (circa 2000) from a friend to take most of the product photographs for the book (see review at *http://www.steves-digicams.com/c2020.html*). Joe also used a 4-MP Canon A80, a fine camera, for the shots taken in the Photosimile 200 light box discussed above. Finally, he used a 3-MP Olympus D-575 point-and-shoot camera (circa 2004) for a few shots. All of these are excellent cameras.

Joe's rules for taking photographs for the book were that he would use the Olympus C-2020 for most of his photographs, and he would not do any post-processing that was not specifically covered in the book.

Joe's constant settings for nearly all of his photographs were:

1. ISO set to 100 for optimal quality without noise.

2. White balance set to Auto.

3. Camera set to aperture priority at f8 to ensure a relatively large depth of field.

So, there you have it. An amateur goes head-to-head with a professional. The rules for the professional are anything goes. The rules for the amateur are restrictive: Use a simple digital camera and only simple post-processing. What's the point of this approach? It is simply to show you that if you follow some basic guidelines, you can take professional-looking product photographs for online use using only inexpensive equipment.

Stanley's Techniques

Keep in mind that Stanley used mass production techniques, as if quickly shooting hundreds of products for a catalog (i.e., appropriate for eBay photography). And at the same time he taught Joe how to take product photographs.

Lights

The incandescent lights used were a pair of Smith Victor 600-watt quartz halogen with a color temperature of 3200K. They were used with umbrellas or with a light tent. The spiral fluorescent lights used were a pair of 26-watt (1600 lumen) with a color temperature of 5000K. (Note that the wattage for incandescent and fluorescent lights are not comparable.) They were used with a light tent or directly for certain small items.

First Rule Last

Here we give the first rule of product photography last. Clean it off! Nobody wants to look at a great photograph of a dirty, begrimed, dusty, or smudged item. Clean it with Windex, water, Pine-Sol, alcohol, acetone, detergent, or packing tape (lint removal). And don't forget a can of compressed gas purchased at a computer supply store for dusting. Even new products often need a little dusting. This is the first step to effective product photography and one you shouldn't skip. And polish the item, too, if it's cost-effective to do so.

7

Small Items - Macro Photography

There are many more small items sold on eBay than larger items. Consequently, small items comprise the main portion of this section of the book. Indeed, there are a number of ways to photograph small items that are generally not used for larger items. For instance, on a tabletop you can use a tent (for diffusion) or a light box for small items. These are generally not used for larger items, although large tents and light boxes are available. But you don't have to use these special devices. You can shoot even the smallest items on a tabletop with photo lights and basic techniques

A Variety of Lighting

This seemed a good chapter to demonstrate a variety of lighting techniques for eBay photography. Everything works with small items. But only stronger lighting works well with large items.

Tent with Incandescent Lighting

A tabletop tent with incandescent lighting works great for small items. You can position two lights in almost any convenient place where they complement each other, such as one on each side of the tent (i.e., each end of the table). The tent we used was an EZcube sold by Table Top Studio LLC (*http://www.ezcube.com*), an exhibitor at eBay Live, the annual eBay conference (see Figure 7.1). Tents are not expensive and are priced according to the size and features.

Figure 7.1 EZcube light tent.

Look at Photo 8, a necklace on a velvet necklace display. The original photograph was OK, but Joe significantly improved it with post-processing using the custom Levels adjustments in Photoshop Elements 3.0.

The bracelet on a piece of black velvet in Photo 9 looks great (Joe used no post-processing). Note that the exposure is one stop under, which reduced some of the specular highlights on this reflective jewelry.

The brooch in Photo 10 was placed on a piece of lavender poster board. The black velvet didn't show the black elements in the brooch well. Joe's version required extensive but quick post-processing.

Note that this lighting was so strong that we were able to take many photographs at high shutter speeds without a tripod.

Fluorescent Lighting

Using fluorescent lighting produced interesting results for several reasons. First, we did not use a diffusion device. Rather, we placed the lights so close to the small items that the lights were larger than the items thereby not requiring a diffusion device (see Chapter 6). Second, the lights had the color temperature of daylight (i.e., 5000K).

To start out, we photographed the two cars (old toys) in the tent with the quarter using the fluorescent lights (see Photo 11), and then Joe used the one-button Levels in the Quick Fix mode of Elements. Then we took the tent off the table and shot one car with the fluorescent lights close in (see Photo 12). Joe's photograph is representative of the item without post-processing.

The necklace looks good without any post-processing (see Photo 13). The bracelet looked OK without any post-processing, but the tan velvet showed the bracelet better when Joe used the custom Levels post-processing in Elements (see Photo 14). We also photographed a small box (see Photos 15 and 16), which turned out OK without any post-processing.

Note that this lighting was weak, and sharp photographs were only possible using a tripod and low shutter speeds.

Light Box

Next we used a light box. We used the MK Digital Direct Photo@Box (*http://www.mkdigitaldirect.com*). This vendor exhibits at eBay Live and is familiar with the needs of eBay businesspeople.

The shots seemed to require post-processing but turned out well. Joe's cars with the quarter looked better after one-button Levels (see Photo 17 and 18). The bracelet looked OK but was enhanced by one-button Levels (see Photo 19). Note the black dots—a reflection of the opening in the top that we didn't close. Embarassing. Joe's brooch turned out well without post-processing. Still, it looked a little more true to color after a one-button Smart Fix (see Photo 20). The mousetrap looked better with one-button Smart Fix too (see Photo 21). The necklace required no post-processing and looked pretty good (see Photo 23 and 24).

Keep in mind that these are all small items. We tried shooting the Milk-Bone metal can in the light box, and it just seemed too big (see Photo 22).

We were impressed by the results from the light box. It works quite well for small items, especially jewelry. If you need to photograph such items routinely, a light box can boost your productivity as well as provide attractive photographs. If you photograph small products only occasionally, you can get by just fine without a light box.

CloudDome

The CloudDome (*http://www.clouddome.com*) is a translucent plastic dome with a hole in the top. You shoot your photographs through the hole with your camera fastened onto a bracket. The dome is quite handy for photographing small things, and a variety of helpful accessories are available to make it more useful. Joe used the dome and an extension collar to photograph a few items. See Photos 59, 72, 73, and 76 appearing at intervals in the center section. The light source was indirect daylight coming through a window.

For the CloudDome itself, you need a camera with good macro capability. The extension collar (an accessory), however, not only provides more volume inside the dome but also allows the use of a camera without super macro capability. CloudDome exhibits at eBay Live.

Macro Photography

Macro capability comes in handy when photographing small items. Joe shot a small portion of the mousetrap in the light box (see Photos 25 and 26) with his Minolta A2 plus two closeup lenses. Joe used one-button Levels and Sharpen for post-processing. The Olympus C-2020 doesn't have a great closeup capability, nor does the Minolta A2. But you can add closeup lenses (inexpensive) to the A2. The fact is that many digital point-and-shoot cameras have better macro capability than either of these two cameras. Still, the Olympus was perfectly adequate, to take a macro shot of the hat in fluorescent lighting (see Photo 28), which looked better with one-button Color post-processing in Elements.

Avoid the Transitional Zone

When using your macro mode, you may find yourself in the transitional zone between needing to use it and not needing to use it. That's a tough place to focus correctly. It's best to set your camera for one mode or the other (set one specific distance) and make other adjustments accordingly to take good photographs.

For instance, you might set your camera on normal mode and then do a substantial crop after taking the photograph. Or you might set it on macro mode and be satisfied with a closer closeup than you had envisioned. Whatever you do, keep out of the transitional zone by setting your camera at a distance that requires it to be put in one mode or the other.

Keep in mind that you will need a tripod to set your camera a specific distance from an item. Photographing without a tripod in the transitional zone can be a disaster.

Your camera dictates what you can do with macro photography. For example, some cameras allow macro mode only at the telephoto end of the zoom or only at wide angle end of the zoom. If the camera allows the macro mode at each end of the zoom, you have much more flexibility. In any event, you will get closer with the telephoto than with the wide angle, and most macro shots look better in telephoto mode.

Also remember the lens perspective factor (see Photos 1 and 2). Telephoto shots appear compressed with a flat look. Wide angle shots appear to have more depth with a risk of unsightly distortion. At the wide angle end of the zoom, you need to be very careful when shooting in the macro mode.

Summary

You can photograph small products, including jewelry, in any kind of photo lighting and get good results. But stick to the basics. Use diffused lighting. Use a neutral backgound or one that enhances the photograph (e.g., velvet for jewelry). Use a tripod. And experiment with the lighting.

Always remember that no post-processing is always better than some post-processing. Your lighting experimentations should lead you to discover setups that will enable you to take good photograph without post-processing. That's the most cost-effective means for your eBay business to become successful and stay successful.

8

Tabletop Items

Tabletop items are small enough to be photographed on your tabletop but too large to be photographed in a tabletop light tent or light box. Size is arbitrary, but anything much larger than a shoe box fits into this category. On the other hand, you don't have to use a light tent or light box for small items, and you can shoot small items on a tabletop too. A prime advantage of working on a tabletop is that it's a good working height. You can sit or stand and do your setting up and shooting comfortably.

Your first task is to set up the background. The roll of seamless paper should be near the ceiling of your studio. Unroll it and bring it down the wall and across to the front of the table. Use three hardware store clamps to fasten it along the front edge of the table. Now you're ready to place the item on the table with a seamless background.

For small items that fit, you can use the CloudDome Infiniti Board (*http://clouddome.com*) for your seamless background. It's convenient if you never shoot larger items.

Also, you can use a large sheet of drawing paper clamped to the front edge of the table and propped up in back with solid props. This is not a durable means of creating a seamless background, but it's OK for occasional use.

Lights

Lights are the key to tabletop shooting just as for all photography. Because the items are large and require more powerful light, the use of strong incandescent lights (e.g., 250-watt to 1000-watt) is recommended. Nonetheless, for smaller items you might want to try spiral fluorescent lights (e.g., 25-watt) and move them in close.

Incandescent Lights

Place the lights with umbrellas or diffusers in the classic position; that is, each 45 degrees offset from the centerline (see Figure 6.8 in Chapter 6). Unfortunately, this is sometimes awkward positioning that gets in your way. You can offset the lights even more to get them out of the way without a significant decline in photographic quality if you use one foam-board reflector in front or two foam-board reflectors, one to each side. Of course, then the reflectors may get in the way. You can also set the lights up high (e.g., six feet) pointed downward to keep them out of the way.

You will need foam-board reflectors at least as large as the item being photographed. For the tabletop, the reflectors might be as large as 30 × 36 inches. We can't tell you where to set the reflectors; that's a matter for experimentation. But the purpose of the reflectors is to add light to any areas of the item that appear dim or are obviously underlit.

Stanley's approach of using one light overhead wasn't appropriate for the old basket backpack. It was too big. Nonetheless, he set up one light from the high right and used a large foam-board reflector on the left (see setup in Figures 8.1 and 8.2). With a 600-watt incandescent light and an umbrella, this was enough lighting for Joe to create good photographs without post-processing (see Photo 29).

Figure 8.1 Setup for photographing tabletop item. Notice the grey seamless paper for the background clamped to the front table edge and the large white foam-board reflector on left side.

This is pretty easy photography. Use strong lights. Use a foam-board reflector to lighten up the dark side of the item. Take some photographs with your camera on a tripod remembering to fill the frame with the item. And you're in business.

Look at Photo 30. With one-button Levels processing the basket pack looks more true to color. But is it worth the extra work?

Figure 8.2 Seamless paper clamped to the front edge of the table.

Fluorescent Lights

Another way to take photographs of smaller tabletop items is with spiral fluorescent lights. Because fluorescent lights are generally weaker than incandescent lights, they don't work as well for large tabletop items unless you use slow shutter speeds (long exposure times). But for smaller tabletop items, you can move the lights in close and take sharp photographs. However, you still need to use foam-board reflectors.

You will see in Photo 66 (also used in Chapter 18) that the Milk-Bone can was lit from each side. Diffusion was accomplished by setting the lights back away from the item. (Note that the lights were not set back very far because the lights were relatively weak.) But because of its shape, the Milk-Bone can has a distinct shadow in the front. Joe should have used a small foam-board reflector to light up the front. But he neglected to do so. Photos 31-33 show the same item placed on the tabletop but in a different position. The lighting is fine even without a foam-board reflector, and Joe's custom adjustment of Brightness/ Contrast looks good (see Photo 33).

The box for the OmniView KVM cables (see Photo 34) shot by Joe looks pretty good without post-processing. It is not difficult to photograph boxes, which is important for eBay retailing, so long as the box has a flat finish. Diffused light does a great job with boxes. For boxes with glossy finishes, however, you will need to be careful that intense specular highlights don't obscure details.

All You Need

Tabletop techniques are all you need. Sure it's great to work with tents and light boxes if you shoot small items all day. If you don't, such equipment can be more trouble than it's worth, particularly for a small studio space. And you can shoot anything small on your tabletop just fine without tents or light boxes.

You don't need a high MP camera either. See the comparison between a 3-MP camera crop and an 8-MP camera crop in Photo 35 and 36. Joe shot these photographs on a tabletop outdoors in the shade of the house. Indeed, a point-and-shoot digital camera and a tabletop is the most popular studio setup and one that provides a lot of flexibility.

For small items, it's worth remembering Stanley's approach. Use one diffused light on a boom beaming from overhead. Then use several foam-board reflectors to light around the bottom of the item. It's simple, it's quick, it's efficient, and it's all you need.

For larger items on the tabletop, Stanley uses one light set up high and one (or more) large foam-board reflector to light the other side of the item. Again, it's efficient with a minimum of costly equipment.

9

Large Items

Large items must be photographed on the floor. Your studio is a suitable place for photographing such items. That is, you can carry them (or roll them) into your studio easily and place them in a position to be photographed. If they are too heavy or too large to be carried easily, you will need to shoot them in place (wherever they are). Large items get the traditional product-photography treatment. That is, you shoot them against a seamless paper background. Items shot in place, of course, come with whatever backgrounds they have.

Setting Up

For floor items, you unroll your seamless background paper from near the ceiling, down the wall and out across the floor. When it's in position, tape it to the floor with gaffer's tape. This doesn't work very well on a carpeted floor, and you are likely to destroy the paper before it wears out. A solid floor is better for your studio if you have a choice. A standard sheet of plywood (4 × 8 feet), or something similarly solid, placed over a carpet will make the use of seamless paper more practical in a permanent studio. If your studio is temporary and your floor carpeted, using seamless background paper may not be practical.

Large items need strong lights. Diffused incandescent lights with significant wattage work best, and large foam-board reflectors are needed as well. Since foam-board comes in 4 × 8 foot sheets, you can create reflectors as large as you need. Still, once reflectors get larger than 30 × 36 inches, they become awkward to use in a studio, and you might consider using several reflectors of that size rather than one larger one. Large reflectors can be propped up with large heavy props.

See Photos 37 and 38 for a chair photographed in a studio on seamless background paper. It looks good and enables potential buyers to see exactly what it is. Joe made an Auto Contrast adjustment in post-processing.

In Place

When you photograph something in place because it's too large or heavy to move into a studio setting, you usually have to decide what you are going to use for lighting. Moving lights to where you need them is likely to be cumbersome and may not be needed. You can often use the available sunlight coming into the room together with foam-board reflectors and low shutter speeds (requiring a tripod) to get good photographs.

Your biggest problem may be figuring out what to do if the background is unacceptable. But you can always crop the item closely keeping out most of the background.

Joe shot the couch in Photo 39. Joe's camera shot a decent photograph with the daylight in the room, foam-board reflectors, and the household incandescent lights turned on. Unfortunately, the color of the couch was not correct. It was only correct when shot with a flash (see Photo 41). Although Joe used the full flash mode, there was so much daylight in the room and the flash on the camera was so weak that the resulting flash had to be considered a fill-in flash. (The only trick in post-processing that worked was changing the tint, which is beyond the scope of this book. See Photo 40.)

Likewise, when Joe shot the wood molding across the top of the couch, the color of the couch was not correct (see Photo 43). Again, standard post-processing could not make a photograph with the correct color. Only when he shot it with the flash (see Photo 44) did he capture the correct color.

In the meantime, Stanley captured the correct color with a fill-in flash. See Photos 42 and 45. Are we recommending that you use a fill-in flash? Not really. What we are recommending is that if you can't get good results with your digital camera in a particular situation, experiment until you find something that works. A fill-in flash may work just fine.

Digital Cameras Allow More Flexibility

When you shoot indoors, perhaps the best approach is to turn on all the readily available lights and open the shutters. Digital cameras allow considerable flexibility in a mixed-light environment in getting a representative photograph. See if that works. If not, you can experiment by adding or subtracting lighting.

In this case, Joe knew right away that he had a problem with the color; he could see it on the LCD screen. He experimented a bit with under-exposures and overexposures, but the technique that worked the best to capture the true color was using a flash. In addition, Joe easily took a colorful photograph of a portion of the carpet (Photo 27) with room light, a flash, and no post-processing.

What could Joe do besides use a flash? Here are some possibilities:

- Use the flash on fill-in mode instead of full mode (i.e., weaker)
- Manually set the white balance.
- Use more foam-board reflectors.
- Use studio lighting.
- Fool around with Tint under Color in the Quick Fix mode (not a process that this book covers)

It's all a matter of experimentation. Use what you've got to make it work.

Conclusion

Large items are easy to shoot well in the studio. If they're in place instead, they're more difficult to shoot and may require a little more experimentation than usual.

10

Clothing

The tough problem with clothing is that it's so limp. You need to turn that limpness into a display with some body, so to speak. You do it with manikins. Don't panic if you don't photograph clothes often. Manikin-like displays are cheap and work well. Manikins and manikin-shaped artifices are not too expensive either and work well for those who sell a lot of clothes. We both feel quite strongly that manikins are a must for eBay clothing photography. Don't set up your studio without one.

Manikins

Manikins come in different sexes and in adults and children. If you sell a lot of clothing, you may need a family of manikins to take your photographs. Fortunately, manikins are not outrageously expensive, and you can find them on eBay between $50 and $200. The objective is not to create an advertising environment for your photographs (unless it's appropriate, in which case see Chapter 23). It's simply to display the clothes you're selling in a way that enables buyers to get a reasonable look at them. It's difficult to evaluate clothing that's flat on the ground, pinned to the wall, or hung on a standard coat hanger. Clothing just doesn't look very good displayed in this way.

Full Manikins

Full manikins are the ones you see in department store windows. They replicate bodies and are appropriate for eBay retailers who sell a lot of clothing.

You can dress, photograph, and undress a manikin quickly. It's more efficient than dealing with a model and more cost-effective, too, even if the model is free (e.g., a relative). By giving some body to your clothes in your eBay photographs, you will sell more clothes for higher prices.

Don't overlook manikin body parts. A head is handy for displaying hats. See Photo 46 and 47 for a hat on a manikin head. The hat looks better on the head than it does flat on the table surface, but the neck shouldn't show. You can use arms and legs for displaying appropriate clothing and accessories.

Manikin Artifices

Some manikin artifices (e.g., dress forms) are not full manikins (i.e., they don't have limbs), but they are fully three-dimensional. They are designed for people who tailor. They make good clothing displays for photographs just as full manikins do. You can find them on eBay for between $50 and $100. However, they have no legs on which to display pants.

Manikin-Like Displays

If you don't photograph clothing often, you can get by with a half-manikin. This is a manikin that is only half three-dimensional and has a hollow open back. It has no arms or legs and has a hanger at the top. You hang it from the ceiling (see Figure 10.1).

Figure 10.1 Half-manikin with a hanger top.

These manikins cost between $10 and $20 on eBay. This is what we used to do the clothing photography for this book.

Shipping

Be aware that the shipping for full manikins and half-manikins tends to be expensive. After all, manikins are life-sized. When buy-

ing a manikin, be sure to check the shipping cost as well as the
price.

See Photos 49 and 50 for a shirt hung on a half-manikin. It doesn't
look great, but it looks much better than a two-dimensional shirt laying flat on the tabletop.

And what about pants? Well, you're out of luck here. It takes a full
manikin to display pants.

Clothing Photography

Photography for clothing is straightforward. Nonetheless, because
clothing has folds, which cause dark crevices, you need to use lighting
carefully or use post-processing. Joe used one-button Smart Fix post-
processing for Photo 49 above. Because clothing is less reflective than
most items, you can even experiment productively with a fill-in flash.

A nice touch is to include a macro shot of the clothing. This often
reveals the texture and character of the fabric for potential buyers to
see. Look at Photo 51, which Joe made without post-processing.

Macro Warning

There is usually a switch to take a digital camera in and out of
macro mode. Any time you switch into macro mode, you don't
want to leave the camera set in macro mode when you go back to
taking normal photographs. You need to remember to switch back.

Some cameras tell you, in effect, that you're still in macro mode
because they stay decidedly out of focus for normal photography.
For other cameras, it's difficult to tell until you look closely at the
normal photographs after the fact. Don't fall into this trap. Pay
attention to what you're doing.

11

Reflective Items

Reflective items are not necessarily more difficult to photograph; you just need to be a little more careful. Remember we said that you should consider each surface of any product as if it were a mirror. The object is to get as few intense specular highlights on each surface as possible. Well, some products are so reflective that they actually are mirrors. You need to be careful that you don't get so much glare that it ruins the photograph.

You have two means available by which to accomplish this. First, use diffused lighting. It's amazing how much glare you can eliminate with diffused lighting. Second, experiment. If you're getting a photograph with too much glare, change the lighting a little and check the LCD screen.

Working with Reflections

In actual shooting, you may experience problems with intense spectral highlights caused by reflective items that you will need to find a way to cure through experimentation.

Post-Processing

Take a look at the chrome cup in Photo 52. The cup looks great in the diffused light (inside a tent, using incandescent lights), but the white balance looks like it might be incorrect. The photograph is too yellow. What can you do about this?

You can set the camera for the proper white balance (i.e., turn off auto white balance). If you shoot other items without a problem, however, and reflective items turn out too yellow, it may be inconvenient to turn off auto white balance.

You can also use post-processing to correct the yellow cast. If you use the one-button Smart Fix in Photoshop Elements 3.0, you get a photograph with less yellow. See Photo 53. It still has a yellowish cast. If you use the one-button Levels in Elements, you should get a photograph without a cast. But you don't. See Photo 54, which still has a yellowish cast. Keep experimenting. If you try the one-button Colors in Elements (see Photo 55), the color is correct, and the photograph looks good. Indeed, with the color adjustment, the photograph of this highly reflective chrome cup looks representative of the real thing.

Daylight

How do you get photographs of reflective products that do not require post-processing? One answer is to shoot them at a daylight color temperature. In this case, we used the tent for diffused light but used two spiral fluorescent lights (with a daylight color temperature). See Photo 56, which is a representative and attractive photograph of the chrome cup. Joe's version required no post-processing.

Wrapping

One thing you may need to photograph often is transparent wrapping (packaging). If a product is inside wrapping, don't rip it open just to photograph it. It's more valuable on eBay if it stays unopened. Shoot it as is and treat it as a reflective item.

In this case, we shot a couple of mousetraps inside a cellophane wrapping without a tent and without diffused lighting. See Photo 57 (no post-processing). We used two spiral fluorescent lights, with a daylight color temperature, that were set very close to the item. (Remember, for closeup lighting where the light source is as big or bigger than the item, you don't need diffusion.)

The wrapped mousetraps are not completely free of intense specular highlights. Note, however, that the intense specular highlights are few in number and do not interfere with the photograph. There is a prominent one at the top of the photograph and along the right side of the wrapping. The photograph remains clear and is representative of the item. You actually want to see some specular highlights on wrapping because it seems natural, so a little is OK. It's only when the specular highlights are so great they burn out the details in the photograph that you need to change your approach.

Glass

To photograph a crystal wine glass, the lights were set up one on each side of the glass at table level. Two small foam-board reflectors were used to reflect light from the front. See Photo 58, the resulting photograph. Joe's version required no post-processing, but with one-button Smart Fix post-processing in Elements, the photograph looks a little different (see Photo 60). Which photograph do you like better? We think that either is OK. Notice that even though the glass is highly reflective, the specular highlights don't overwhelm it. Sure, you can eliminate even more glare if you want to experiment with lights and foam-board reflectors all day. But this setup and photography was done quickly.

Anti-Reflector?

We've mentioned white foam-board reflectors as being handy to light dimly lit areas in a setup for a photograph. How about using black foam-board or black drawing paper to reduce glare? Yes, it works. Try it. Experiment with black just like you experiment with a reflector.

Conclusion

Diffused light shows reflective products well. You may have a problem occasionally when the auto white balance on your camera doesn't work for reflective items resulting in a yellowish cast. You can set the white balance manually, use post-processing to correct the yellow cast, or use lights with a daylight color temperature. The bottom line is that reflective items can be photographed as efficiently as other eBay items.

Color Photographs

Any products depicted in the photographs herein are being used as examples only and do not in any way suggest an affiliation, sponsorship or approval by the owner of the trademarks appearing on such products. All trademarks are owned by their respective companies.

Photo 1 Wide angle zoom in overcast sky (Joe – Olympus D-575 – custom Levels – Auto Sharpen).

Photo 2 Telephoto zoom in overcast sky (Joe – Olympus D-575 – custom Levels – Auto Sharpen).

Photo 3 Sunny sky (Joe – Minolta A2 – custom Levels – custom Shadows/Highlights – custom Brightness/Contrast – Auto Sharpen).

Photo 4 Overcast sky (Joe – Olympus D-575 – no post-processing).

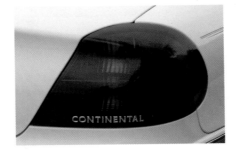

Photo 5 Overcast sky (Joe – Olympus D-575 – no post-processing).

Photo 6 Sunny sky (Joe – Olympus D-575 – no post-processing).

Photo 7 Sunny sky (Joe – Olympus D-575 – no post-processing). The shady side of the truck in Photo 6.

Photo 8 Tent with incandescent light (Left: Joe – Olympus C-2020 – custom Levels) (Right: Stanley – Fuji F-700 – post-processing).

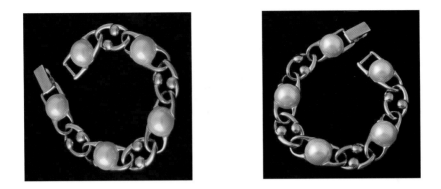

Photo 9 Tent with incandescent light (Left: Joe – Olympus C-2020 – no post-processing) (Right: Stanley – Fuji F-700 – post-processing).

Photo 10 Tent with incandescent light (Left: Joe – Olympus C-2020 – Auto Levels – Auto Color – Auto Sharpen) (Right: Stanley – Nikon D70 – no post-processing).

Photo 11 Tent with fluorescent light (Joe – Olympus C-2020 – Auto Levels – Auto Sharpen).

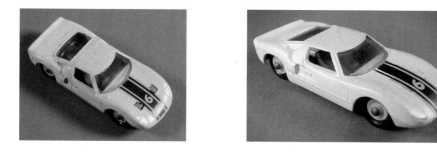

Photo 12 Direct fluorescent light (Left: Joe – Olympus C-2020 – no post processing) (Right: Stanley – Fuji F-700 – post-processing).

Photo 13 Direct fluorescent light (Joe – Olympus C-2020 – no post-processing).

Photo 14 Direct fluorescent light (Left: Joe – Olympus C-2020 – custom Levels) (Right: Stanley – Fuji F-700 – no post-processing).

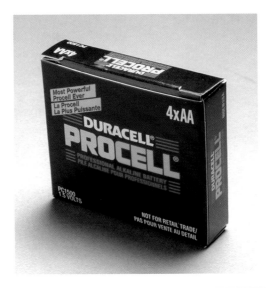

Photo 15 Direct fluorescent light (Joe – Olympus C-2020 – no post-processing).

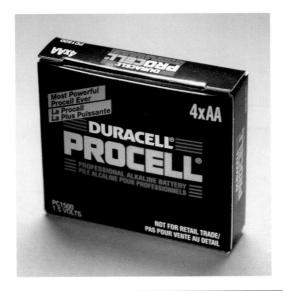

Photo 16 Direct fluorescent light (Stanley – Fuji F-700 – no post-processing).

Photo 17 Light box (Joe – Olympus C-2020 – Auto Smart Fix).

Photo 18 Light box (Stanley – Nikon D70 – post-processing).

Photo 19 Light box (Joe – Olympus C-2020 – Auto Levels – Auto Sharpen).

Photo 20 Light box (Left: Joe – Olympus C-2020 – Auto Smart Fix) (Right: Stanley – Fuji F-700 – post-processing).

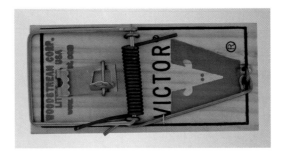

Photo 21 Light box (Joe – Olympus C-2020 – Auto Smart Fix).

Photo 22 MK Digital Direct light box.

Photo 23 Light box (Joe – Olympus C-2020 – no post-processing).

Photo 24 Light box (Stanley – Nikon D70 – no post-processing).

Photo 25 Light box macro (Joe – Minolta A2 + two closeup lenses – Auto Levels – Auto Sharpen).

Photo 26 Light box macro (Stanley – Fuji F-700 – post-processing).

Photo 27 Room light with flash (Joe – Olympus C-2020 – no post-processing).

Photo 28 Fluorescent light macro (Left: Joe – Olympus C-2020 – Auto Color – custom Sharpen) (Right: Stanley – Fuji F-700 – no post-processing).

Photo 29 Incandescent light (Left: Joe – Olympus C-2020 – no post-processing) (Right: Stanley – Nikon D70 – post-processing).

Photo 30 Incandescent light (Joe – Olympus C-2020 – Auto Levels – Auto Sharpen).

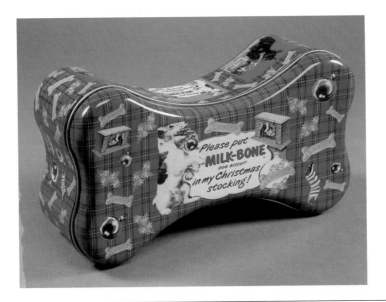

Photo 31 Fluorescent light (Joe – Olympus C-2020 – no post-processing).

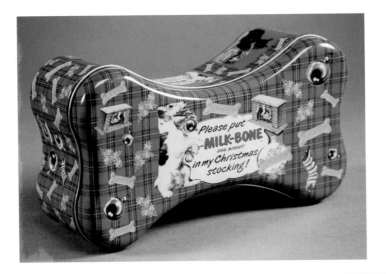

Photo 32 Fluorescent light (Stanley – Nikon D70 – post-processing).

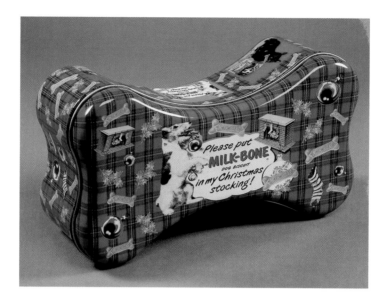

Photo 33 Fluorescent light (Joe – Olympus C-2020 – custom Brightness/ Contrast – Auto Sharpen).

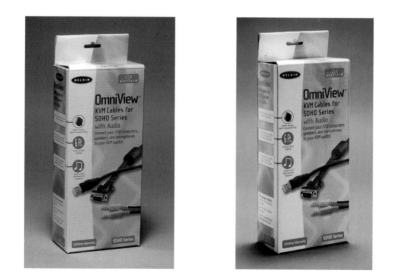

Photo 34 Fluorescent light (Joe – Olympus C-2020 – no post-processing) (Stanley – Nikon D70 – post-processing).

Photo 35 Sunny sky in the shade of the house (Joe – Minolta A2 – custom Levels – custom Shadows/Highlights – custom Sharpen).

Photo 36 Each is a cropped three-percent section of its original full photograph identical to Photo 35, both with custom Levels and custom Sharpening (Left: Joe – 3-MP Olympus D-575) (Right: Joe – 8-MP Minolta A2).

Photo 37 Incandescent light (Joe – Olympus C-2020 – Auto Brightness/Contrast – Auto Sharpen).

Photo 38 Incandescent light (Stanley – Nikon D70 – post-processing).

Photo 39 Daylight in room (Joe – Olympus C-2020 – no post-processing).

Photo 40 Daylight in room (Joe – Olympus C-2020 – custom Tint – Auto Sharpen).

Photo 41 Daylight in room with flash (Joe – Olympus C-2020 – no post-processing).

Photo 42 Daylight in room with fill-in flash (Stanley – Nikon D70 – no post-processing).

Photo 43 Daylight in room (Joe – Olympus C-2020 – no post-processing).

Photo 44 Daylight in room with flash (Joe – Olympus C-2020 – no post-processing).

Photo 45 Daylight in room with fill-in flash (Stanley – Fuji F-700 – no post-processing).

Photo 46 Fluorescent light (Joe – Olympus C-2020 – Auto Contrast – Auto Sharpen).

Photo 47 Fluorescent light (Stanley – Fuji F-700 – post-processing).

Photo 48 Photosimile 200 light box (Joe – Canon A80 – no post-processing).

Photo 49 Fluorescent light (Joe – Olympus C-2020 – Auto Smart Fix).

Photo 50 Fluorescent light (Stanley – Fuji F-700 – post-processing).

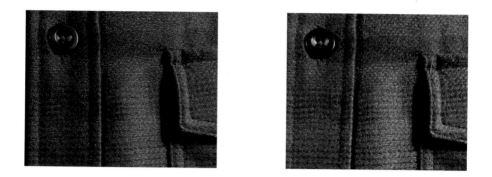

Photo 51 Fluorescent light (Left: Joe – Olympus C-2020 – no post-processing) (Right: Stanley – Fuji F-700 – post-processing).

Photo 52 Incandescent light (Joe – Olympus C-2020 – no post-processing).

Photo 53 Incandescent light (Joe – Olympus C-2020 – Auto Smart Fix).

Photo 54 Incandescent light (Joe – Olympus C-2020 – Auto Levels).

Photo 55 Incandescent light (Joe – Olympus C-2020 – Auto Color).

Photo 56 Tent with fluorescent light (Left: Joe – Olympus C-2020 – no post-processing) (Right: Stanley – Nikon D70 – post-processing)).

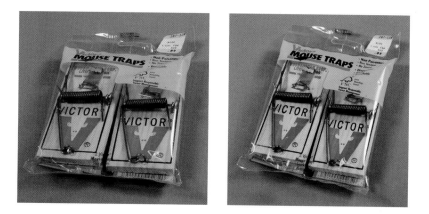

Photo 57 Fluorescent light (Left: Joe – Olympus C-2020 – no post-processing) (Right: Stanley – Nikon D70 – no post-processing).

Photo 58 Fluorescent light (Left: Joe – Olympus C-2020 – no post-processing) (Right: Stanley – Nikon D70 – post-processing).

Photo 59 CloudDome with daylight (Joe – Olympus D-575 – no post-processing).

Photo 60 Fluorescent light (Joe – Olympus C-2020 – Auto Smart Fix).

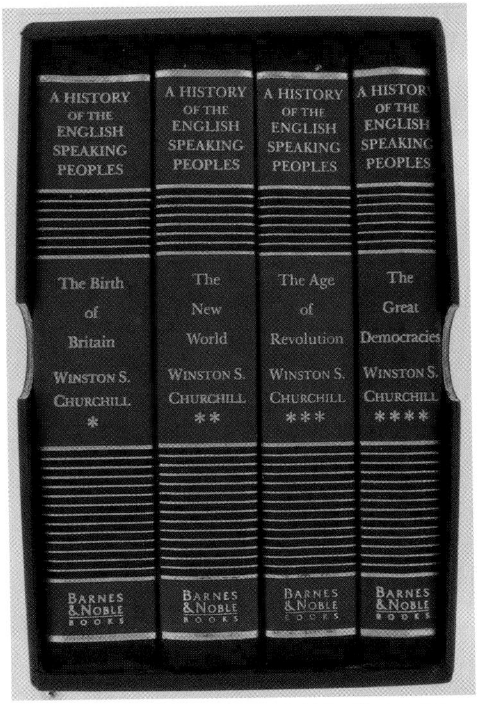

Photo 61 Photosimile 200 light box (Joe – Canon A80 – no post-processing).

Photo 62 Fluorescent light (Joe – Olympus C-2020 – no post-processing).

Photo 63 Fluorescent light (Stanley – Nikon D70 – post-processing).

Photo 64 Fluorescent light (Joe – Olympus C-2020 – no post-processing).

Photo 65 Fluorescent light (Joe – Olympus C-2020 – no post-processing).

Photo 66 Sunny sky in the shade of the house (Joe – Olympus D-575 – no post-processing).

Photo 67 Sunny sky in the shade of the house (Joe – Olympus D-575 – custom Levels – custom Sharpen).

Photo 68 Fluorescent light (Joe – Olympus C-2020 – no post-processing).

Photo 69 Fluorescent light (Joe – Olympus C-2020 – Auto Levels – custom Shadows/Highlights – custom Brightness/Contrast – Auto Sharpen).

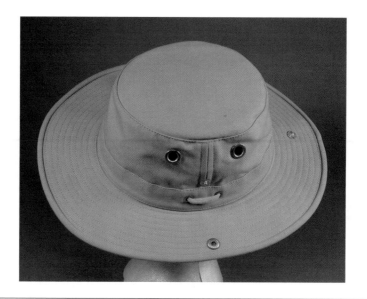

Photo 70 Fluorescent light (Joe – Olympus C-2020 – no post-processing).

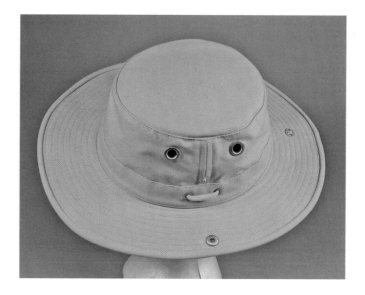

Photo 71 Fluorescent light (Joe – Olympus C-2020 – custom Shadows/ Hightlights – Auto Sharpen).

Photo 72 CloudDome with daylight (Left: Joe – Olympus D-575 – Auto Smart Fix) (Right: Joe – Olympus D-575 – Auto Levels – Auto Sharpen). A tent, light box, or CloudDome is your alternative for shooting small graphics rather than posting them on the wall and beaming lights on them.

Photo 73 CloudDome with daylight (Joe – Olympus D-575 – Auto Levels – Auto Sharpen). You can get a detailed and attractive photograph quickly and easily with a tent, light box, or Cloud-Dome. Black is often difficult to photograph. This is an old point-and-shoot film camera.

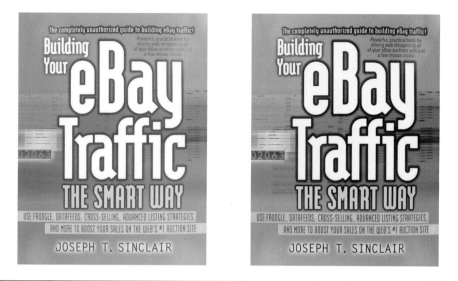

Photo 74 Photosimile 200 light box (Left: Joe – Canon A80 – no post-processing) (Right: Joe – Canon A80 – Auto Smart Fix). The original is just a little washed out. You can cure that with post-processing or shooting one-half stop, or more, underexposed.

Photo 75 Photosimile 200 light box (Joe – Canon A80 – no post-processing). This is one-half stop underexposed and requires no post-processing. Compare it to the post-processed photograph above.

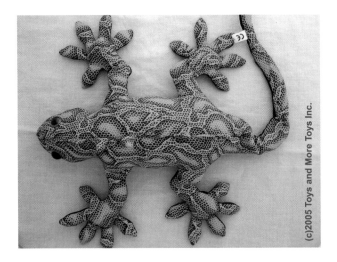

Photo 76 CloudDome with daylight (Joe – Olympus D-575 – Auto Levels – Auto Color – Auto Sharpen). Note the copyright notice.

Photo 77 Sunny sky in the shade of the house (Joe – 3-MP Canon A70 – custom Brightness/ Contrast – custom Sharpen). This is one of the photographs that helped Joe sell his Minolta film camera and lenses in 2003 for a high price on eBay.

See Shooting for the Book in Chapter 6 for general information
on how the photographs were taken by Joe and Stanley.

12

Graphics

Photographing graphics, otherwise known as two-dimensional art, takes a special technique. Perhaps a better description is that it takes a special setup. If you get set up correctly, the photography is straightforward. Shooting graphics requires two lights placed equidistant from the wall, each on a line 45 degrees offset from the centerline (one left and one right) at the same height as the item, assuming the item is posted vertically. Precision is important in shooting graphics.

Your first question might be, Why post the graphic vertically? It seems more difficult than just laying the item flat and photographing it from above. Indeed, if the items you shoot are always small (i.e., less than 24 × 24 inches) and you shoot in volume, you might consider setting up your equipment to have your camera shoot from overhead at items laying flat on a table. (This is one situation where an articulating LCD screen will come in handy. See Chapter 2.) If you have items larger than 24 × 24 to shoot, however, they are simply too large for most tabletop setups.

Posting

How do you post a graphic on a vertical wall? As invisibly as you can. In other words, whatever you use to attach the graphic to the wall, you want it to be as invisible as possible in the photograph. You can use Scotch tape, gaffers tape, pins, push pins, or even magnets. You might have a smooth wall where you use tape, a cork (or wood) wall where you use push pins, or a steel wall where you use magnets. You work around the edges of the item. Naturally, your posting wall needs to be larger than 24 × 24, or you might as well use a tabletop setup instead.

Posting Horizontally

Sometimes when you use a tabletop setup, you don't have to worry about posting (attaching) the graphic to the table because it lays flat. At other times, you will find that the graphic is warped and must be pinned down, so to speak, to make it lay flat.

You can purchase special tabletop setups for shooting graphics that include a means of flattening a graphic and brackets to set lights at the proper angle and distance.

If an item includes a graphic but is not itself a graphic, you don't necessarily need to shoot it as a graphic. For instance, a DVD case is flat and has a colorful advertising graphic on it. Don't shoot it as a graphic. Prop it up and shoot it like any other product. It will be mostly a graphic, but it will also be a photograph of the DVD case. If you get too much glare from the graphic on the case, remember the principles of this chapter and adjust your setup according.

Setup

First, you need a visible centerline running from the top of the wall to the bottom of the wall and then out across the floor. When you post your item, center it on the centerline and level it with a bubble level. Your tripod needs to place your camera lens on the centerline at exactly the same height as the center of the graphic. Your two lights need to be equidistant from the wall, offset on a line 45 degrees from the centerline (one to the left and one to the right), and at the same height as the center of the graphic.

Use a tape measure to get the distances correct. Each light should be equidistant from the centerline, equidistant from the wall, and at the same height as the center of the graphic. Your camera lens should be on the centerline at the same height as the center of the graphic.

Look at Photos 62 and 63 (no post-processing for Joe's version). The setup is perfect. There's no glare. You can see the centerline. You can also see that the item is posted slightly off horizontal. We should have used a bubble level.

Horizontal Adjustment

You can adjust this record album cover to be perfectly horizontal in Photoshop Elements. But that's an extra post-processing step you don't want to have to take if you don't need to. It's better to use a bubble level to get it horizontal in the first place.

Now look at Photo 64, which was not set up correctly. The glare from the light ruins the photograph. Also look at Photo 65. The setup is fine except that the camera is below the height of the center of the item. The item is no longer a square. Precision is the name of the game when photographing graphics.

You might also note that this item was posted on a bulletin board with push pins. This is a quick and easy way to post, but with a little imagination you might come up with something that's more invisible.

Summary

A tape measure is your best tool in getting set up to photograph graphics. Be precise, and you will be able to shoot without intense specular highlights.

13

Enhanced Presentations

We will discuss in the next chapter (Outdoor Photography) that you need to ensure that the background for outdoor photographs is appropriate and non-distractive. After all, you can't use seamless background paper to create a neutral background for a car, so you need to create something else. But we also warn that creating an advertising environment (as covered in Chapter 23) for photographs is not normally cost-effective. And therein lies the problem. How far can you go towards creating an enhanced photographic environment for shooting eBay items without it becoming an advertising effort and thus losing its cost-effectiveness?

We say you can't go very far, yet certain types of items call for a little more than the standard studio treatment. Items that have an aesthetic purpose particularly need special consideration. For instance, jewelry and clothing have an aesthetic purpose. They exist to make people look good. Therefore, they need an enhanced presentation to bring out their true character and their attractiveness.

That's where props come in. It is worth taking a little of your time to use some inexpensive props to display certain items. We have already seen some of these props in prior chapters. Let's make a list of some of the things you can use as props or to assemble props:

- Manikins and simulated manikins

- Jewelry displays

- Coat hangers

- Gaffers tape, putty, and museum gel

- Hooks

- Clamps

- Bottles

Manikins

The easiest and best way to display clothing is on a manikin. But what about a person? A person is OK, too, but as soon as you get a second person involved in the photographic process, cost-effectiveness tends to evaporate. If you hire a real model, the cost skyrockets. But one person can dress a manikin quickly and shoot the photographs, and manikins make clothing look attractive. This is particularly important because clothing is otherwise difficult to photograph.

Jewelry Displays

Jewelry displays come in different sizes and shapes (see Figure 13.1). They consist of a shape covered with black velvet.

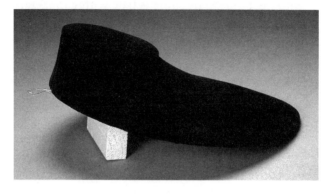

Figure 13.1 Jewelry display for under $10.

Jewelry displays are very reasonably priced. Try Fetpak (*http://www.fetpak.com*) for a selection. You can find them on eBay too. Use them for jewelry. Some you can even use for other items. Take the unsightly lint off the black velvet with pieces of packing tape. In addition, many jewelry boxes make good props for shooting jewelry.

Coat Hangers

Coat hangers are great, but not because they're for hanging clothes. Use them as stiff but bendable wire to make custom displays for items. Of course, construct such displays so that the coat hanger wire cannot be seen in the photographs.

Note that we used an inexpensive polystyrene manikin head to photograph a hat (see Photo 46). Instead, we could have made a hat display prop from a coat hanger. A hat photographed lying on a flat surface doesn't look very exciting. It looks better on a display prop.

Sticky Stuff

Gaffers tape is similar to duct tape except the adhesive doesn't come off as easily to mess things up. As we all know, you can do anything with duct tape. The same is true with gaffers tape. It's great for assembling display props for items or holding items in place. Putty makes a stable support for small things and will also hold things in place. Clear museum gel is like putty but not as strong. (Wondering where to get gaffers tape or museum gel? Try eBay!)

Hooks in the Ceiling

Hooks in the ceiling above your table come in handy for many different purposes, such as hanging an inexpensive half-manikin.

Clamps

Clamps are handy for assembling special displays, clamping down seamless background paper, and so forth. You can buy a variety of clamps inexpensively at a hardware store. Also keep in mind that clothespins can double as clamps.

Bottles

Bottles with flat bottoms that are filled with water, sand, rocks, or chocolate raisins make stable props (if you don't eat the raisins). Gatorade bottles are a good example. You will need a variety of sizes. For instance, use a bottle to prop up a book. It's easier than photographing it laying flat.

Summary

For things that require an enhanced display, such as jewelry, buy some inexpensive displays or assemble displays using inexpensive materials. But make sure what you're doing is cost-effective.

IV

Product Photography Outdoors

14

Photography Outdoors

It's the same old photographic problem outdoors as indoors. It's the light! Only outdoors you can't control it. Instead, you have to work around it—or wait for it. Ah, yes. Those bright sunny days are great. But what about those dreary overcast days? They're kind of depressing, but for product photography they can be great. It's the sunny days that may be too harsh; that is, they may cause too much glare. It's all about diffusion. You need diffused light outdoors, just as you do indoors, in order to get solid product photographs with sharp details that aren't bleached out by intense specular highlights.

So what's the best advice we can give you about shooting items outdoors? Wait for an overcast day. An overcast sky provides you the diffusion you need to take good product photographs. It's that simple.

Now, keep in mind we're not doing landscapes here where we show the sky. We're photographing products that fill the frame. If the overcast sky shows at all, it should show as a minor part of the background. The diffused light of an overcast day enables you to take photographs with sharp details and no glare—and perhaps no post-processing. What a great deal!

Indoor Outdoors

Who is to say you can't take your indoor photography outdoors on an overcast day or in the shade of your house on a sunny day? As long as it isn't raining or windy, you might be able to achieve greater efficiency shooting outdoors than indoors. If you have an eBay business where you can do your photographs in batches several times a month, you might develop a strategy of waiting for overcast days with otherwise good weather and shooting outside.

If you do shoot your indoor photography outdoors, you will need a portable studio that you can efficiently set up and take down. You will still need seamless background paper, a table, foam-board reflectors, and the like.

Products

What type of products do you shoot outdoors? Big ones. The stuff you can't easily bring indoors to photograph and the stuff that's too big to photograph indoors even though it may be stored indoors. A car makes a good example. It's almost impossible to photograph it in the garage; there's not enough room. You need to move it outside and shoot it in the daylight.

A car is easy to move out of the garage, but what about a canoe? Suppose you have a canoe hung from the ceiling in your garage. It would be impractical to photograph it there to show the details. You need to move it outside first. By moving it outside onto the lawn, you can take useful photographs quickly and efficiently. Getting set up to shoot inside with a neutral background would be much more trouble than shooting it on the lawn (or on two sawhorses above the snow in winter).

You will find most large outdoor products more convenient to shoot outdoors unless you create an indoor studio especially designed to handle large products.

Sunlight

One benefit of shooting outside is that you may be able to get by without a tripod. The sun is pretty strong even on an overcast sky. Hand-held photography can go much faster than tripod photography so long as you can shoot at high shutter speeds.

Dark Days

We all know, however, that some overcast days are darker than others. Certainly it can get quite dark on a terribly overcast day. That doesn't necessarily mean that the wonderful diffused light is gone. It may only mean that you will have to use lower shutter speeds and a tripod. Even though the diffused light isn't as intense, you may still be able to take advantage of it.

Sunny Days

When the day is sunny and you have to shoot, what do you do? You shoot with the sun behind you (but not directly behind you), and you monitor the intense specular highlights.

Shooting with the sun behind you may require that you move the item during the photography session. For instance, suppose you need to photograph a car from each side: left, right, front, and back. In order to keep the sun behind you for each shot, you will have to move the car accordingly. This is not necessary on an overcast day.

You will also need to be careful of the intense specular highlights on the car. You don't want them to burn out significant details in the photograph. So review each photograph on your camera's LCD screen after you shoot to determine the extent of the specular highlights.

If you can control the intense specular highlights so that they create sparkles instead of large patches of glare, you can actually take an appealing photograph in direct sunlight (see Photo 3). But you may have to work at it a bit to get it right. Try underexposing by a stop or even two stops to bring specular highlights under control.

In the Shadows

Another approach is to work cleverly. Create the effect of an overcast day on a sunny day by working in the shadows. For example, move a car into the shadow of a house or garage if possible. All that's in the shadow is diffused light. You may have to use a tripod and you may even need reflectors or a fill-in flash, but shooting in the shadows can be done productively and efficiently with great results.

If you're in a place with perpetual sunshine and good weather (e.g., the West), you can shoot outside regularly in the shadows. If you're in a place with perpetual overcast (e.g., the East), you can shoot outside regularly anywhere so long as there's no rain and wind.

Backgrounds

There's no seamless background paper outside. You have to make sure the background for your photograph is appropriate and non-distractive. For instance, when you shoot a car, shoot it in a pleasant subdivision, not an industrial area. When you shoot a forklift, shoot it in an attractive industrial area, not a housing subdivision. In any event, make sure the background doesn't distract from the item.

There are three ways to avoid distraction. First, experiment with your shots. Second, fill the frame with the item. You're not selling the background; you're selling the item. If you fill the frame with the item, there won't be much background to worry about.

Third, for large items, you have to stand back somewhat to get the item in the frame. You don't need as large a depth of field as you do when shooting products close up. Therefore, open the aperture to get a smaller depth of field. By photographing a car with a shallow depth of field, you can keep the car in focus but have the background out of focus. It takes a little experimentation to get it right, but a blurry background normally isn't distractive.

Also note that you can use the ground as a background. Get a stepladder, climb to the top, and shoot down toward the ground. This gives you another angle on such items as motorcycles and boats.

Action?

Keep in mind, I am not advocating an advertising background as covered in Chapter 23. Outside, you are stuck without a neutral background. You have to make the best of it. You can make the best of it by keeping the background appropriate and non-distractive without going to the extra time and effort of using a background that helps sell the item.

Let's face it: The best way to sell an item is to provide a photograph of the item in action. For an SUV (e.g., Land Rover), you will want to shoot it racing down a dirt road, a rooster tail of dust flying up in the air behind it, and sandstone canyon walls in the background. Hey, that's a tough photograph to take, even if you're an expert. Might take a couple of days of hard shooting to get it right. And then what do you have?

What you have is a photograph that sells SUVs but not your particular SUV. You still need to provide detailed photographs of your SUV, showing its true condition, to induce a prospective buyer to make a purchasing decision.

So action is great, but it's out of our league as eBay sellers and photographers. Stick with providing potential buyers with photographs they can use to carefully inspect the item you offer for sale. As a practical matter, that's all you can do, and fortunately that's all you need to do.

First Rule Last

Here we will give the first rule of product photography last. Where have you heard this before? Clean it off! Nobody wants to look at a great photograph of a grungy item. For most outdoor items, cleaning is a big job, but it's one we're used to doing from time to time if not regularly. Take the time to wash, clean, and polish.

You can wash and wax a car. Or you can take the dirt off and make it look glossy in Photoshop Elements. It will take you ten minutes to wash and wax the car at a car wash. It will take you ten hours to remove the dirt and make the car glossy in Elements. Your choice.

15

Outdoor Items

There's nothing so flexible for photography as having plenty of light, and daylight provides about as much as you will ever get. So the primary question is, How can you find diffused light? And the answer is, experiment. Alas, you have no control over the weather, and sometimes shooting at the best site is inconvenient. For instance, what if the nearest shade big enough for the car you need to photograph is on the side drive by your cousin's big house 25 miles away? That might be too inconvenient. You might have to shoot near your house in the bright sun.

129

Experiment

Photographing items outdoors is no different than indoors. Be ready to experiment with the light. Don't forget two techniques that may help: foam-board reflectors and a fill-in flash. Outside you may even find it productive to use professional collapsible reflectors. But for most outdoor photography, you won't need any of these.

In the Sun

Many outdoor items are highly reflective, such as cars, tractors, and boats. Indeed, vehicles are shiny, and the sun causes intense specular highlights. But if you can take a photograph that puts the specular highlights in the right places, you can get a spectacular photograph, so to speak.

Look at Photo 3 (a car Joe purchased on eBay for $7,800). The specular highlights are almost too much, but not quite. The highlights have been toned down during post-processing by adjusting Shadow/Highlights in Photoshop Elements 3.0. This post-processing together with custom Levels and custom Brightness/Contrast adjustments have turned the intense specular highlights into sparkles, which give the car an attractive look. You wouldn't want the photograph to have more sparkle than this, but some sparkle for certain car shots may help your sales.

Closeups

When doing closeups (e.g., to show defects) on a sunny day, shoot into the shadow of the car itself where possible to avoid glare from the sun.

Diffused Daylight

Look at Photo 4 of the same car shot at a different time with an overcast sky. No sparkle, but the car shows lots of detail without any post-processing. Photo 5 (no post-processing) shows a closeup of the car without specular highlights. You may want the sparkle for the overall shots, but you want to show sharp details in the closeup shots. After all, you take the closeups to show defects or attractive details, and you don't want specular highlights to interfere.

In Place

There may come a time when you have to photograph items outdoors that can't be moved. For example, Joe agreed to shoot an old 1946 International pickup truck body (no engine) for a friend for eBay. It wasn't movable. You sometimes have to make do with whatever situation presents itself and make the best of it regardless of the diffused or undiffused status of the sun. In such situations, consciousness of the available light and experimentation with your camera become your most useful techniques (see Photo 6 with the sun behind camera). Nonetheless, there's only so much you can do sometimes unless you wait until the sun is in a different place in the sky (see Photo 7 with the sun in front of camera).

Buildings

eBay has a robust real estate market, and you may find yourself shooting a building someday. Here are some tips to remember:

- The higher the building, the more the vertical lines will tend to converge toward the top. There's not much you can do about multistory buildings, but for single-story buildings, get as far away as is practical so that convergence is less noticeable. Also remember that telephoto shots show less distortion than wide angle shots.

- Keep the plane of the camera's sensor parallel to the vertical plane of the building. By using a tripod, you can step away from the camera to observe whether the camera is level and pointed straight at the building.

- If you take photographs of all sides of a building, visit it at different times of day in order to take photographs as often as possible with the sun behind you (but not directly behind you). If you take photographs on an overcast day, do it on a light overcast day. Dark overcast days don't work well for buildings.

- Crop a building photograph closely, particularly when the photograph shows an overcast sky. It may be OK to take photographs on a light overcast day, but no one wants to see the overcast in the photograph.

- Take photographs just before or after dawn, or at dusk, when sunlight is very soft (diffused). But the glow must come from behind you, not from behind the building. In addition, the glow will have a color cast that must be compatible with your photography.

Every building is different. If the photograph is an important one, spend some time observing the building to determine at what time of day it looks best and photograph it then. Stanley does a lot of architectural photography. Sometimes he plans his shoots six months in advance to take the photographs at just the right time of year. This will probably not be necessary for you, but it reinforces the idea that sometimes the best photographs of a building are shot at a time during the day when it looks the best.

Summary

You have plenty to work with outdoors. Sunlight is particularly strong whether undiffused or diffused. It's not a matter of creating the proper light; it's simply a matter of working with it. And that's what cameras and photographers do best. So experiment, and see what you can do with what you have to work with each day.

V

Workflow for Digital Processing

16

Basic Processing

The point, of course, is to take such good photographs that you don't need any post-processing. No system and no photographer is perfect, however, and post-processing can save you the time and effort of rephotographing.

The post-processing for this book was done with Adobe Photoshop Elements 3.0. Although many other competing programs are adequate as well, this program was chosen for its robust capabilities and its reasonable price. Indeed, it has much of the capability of Adobe Photoshop CS, the leading graphics editor.

The Basics

We define the *basic* digital functions for processing digital photographs as follows:

- Cropping

- Levels

- Saturation

- Brightness and Contrast

- Resizing

- Sharpening

We also cover an additional function in Chapter 18. These functions will go a long way toward correcting your marginal photographs assuming you took the photographs carefully in the first place.

Preview Box

Notice that many function panels have a preview box. If it is checked, you will get an instant preview of any adjustment you make. If not, you won't.

The Goal

You are not a fine arts photographer. The goal is to present the item to potential buyers for inspection to help them make a purchase decision. Keep in mind that post-processing is extra work that is usually unnecessary if you're careful in the first place. But when you need it, you need it. So here it is.

Cropping

The thing of primary importance in your photograph is the item. Shoot your photograph so that the item fills the frame. When you get a shot where the item does not fill the frame, however, you can use the cropping tool in post-processing to correct the photograph. But keep in mind also that cropping does not work well automatically. It requires custom attention. In other words, it doesn't work well for batch processing.

Cropping is quite easy, and every image editor has a cropping capability. Cropping is the first step in your post-processing workflow (see Figure 16.1).

Figure 16.1 A photograph cropped.

Levels

In the recent past, brightness and contrast adjustments were your best bet to improve a photograph. Levels, which normally work better, were not available in low-cost image editors. Now you can use levels in Photoshop Elements 3.0 and dispense with the need to adjust brightness and contrast most of the time.

For custom levels adjustment, you must adjust the input levels for each color channel separately. In Elements, go Enhance, Adjust Lighting, Levels. You will get the panel below (see Figure 16.2).

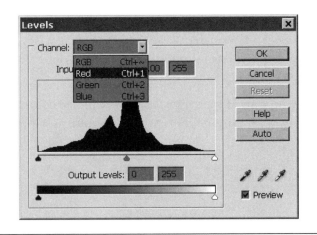

Figure 16.2 Levels panel in Photoshop Elements 3.0.

Pick one of the three colors: red, green, or blue. Now you have a custom levels panel (see Figure 16.3).

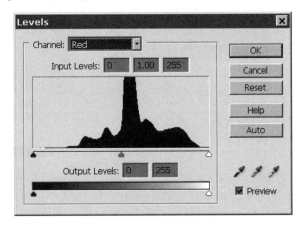

Figure 16.3 Levels panel for red.

Notice the white arrowhead along the bottom of the graph on the right and the black arrowhead on the left. Your job is to move those to the edge of the color input registration. When you're done, it should look like Figure 16.4.

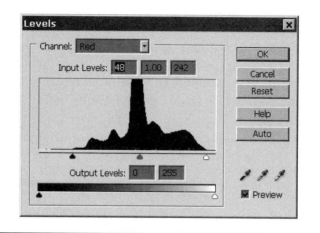

Figure 16.4 Levels adjustments set for red.

Next, do the same for green and blue. Then you're done. Your photograph should look better with colors that are truer to reality. In some cases, your photograph will look much better (see Photos 66 and 67).

Saturation

Color saturation isn't always a must. However, if the colors look a little more pale than you would like, you can boost the saturation to make the colors richer and more vibrant. Go Enhance, Adjust Color, Hue/Saturation to get the panel (see Figure 16.5).

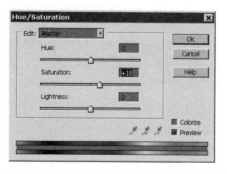

Figure 16.5 Hue/Saturation panel.

Brightness and Contrast

Adjusting brightness and contrast is a fallback technique. If adjusting levels doesn't work, you might try experimenting with brightness and contrast adjustments. A little decrease in brightness and a little increase in contrast works to improve many photographs (see Photo 33), but it depends on so many factors that you will have to experiment. Go Enhance, Adjust Lighting, Brightness/Contrast (see panel in Figure 16.6).

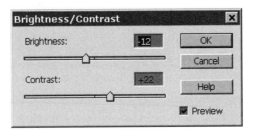

Figure 16.6 Brightness/Contrast panel.

Resizing

Once you have made your adjustments, you need to resize. We recommend that your eBay product photographs be about 400 pixels wide. You don't want them to be larger because they will take too long to download. If they're smaller, prospective buyers may not be able to see what they need to see. Go Image, Image Size, Resize (see Figure 16.7). In the panel, enter 400 for the width. Make sure the mode is set to pixels. Elements will automatically adjust the height to maintain the aspect ratio (ratio of width to height). If the aspect ratio is not maintained during resizing, the photograph will become distorted.

Don't use resize to make an image larger. You should always work with an image too large and reduce it. Don't start with one too small and enlarge it. It just doesn't work well.

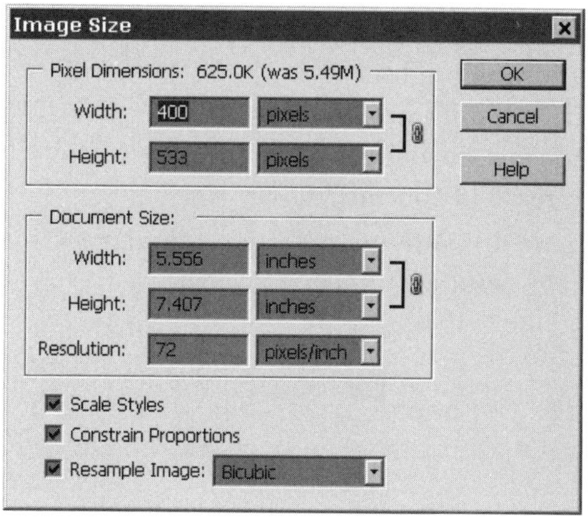

Figure 16.7 Resize image panel.

Sharpening

Do the sharpening for the size image you intend to use. If you sharpen
for a 1200 × 1600 image and then reduce it to 400 × 533, the sharpening will lose its effect. Therefore, always do your sharpening after you
do your resizing. Go Filter, Sharpen, Unsharp Mask (see panel in Figure 16.8).

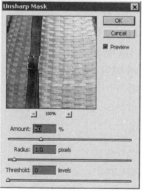

Figure 16.8 Unsharp Mask sharpening filter panel.

You can sharpen from 1 to 500 percent. Start with 50 percent and experiment. Be careful not to over-sharpen. Over-sharpening can give an otherwise good photograph a crazy look. Usually 100 percent is enough, although occasionally a photograph will look best with 200 percent or even higher.

There are other ways to sharpen using the Sharpen filter. Don't use them. Stick with Unsharp Mask.

Automation

You don't have to do custom processing. You can use automation in the Quick Fix mode instead. See the Quick Fix menu in Figure 16.9.

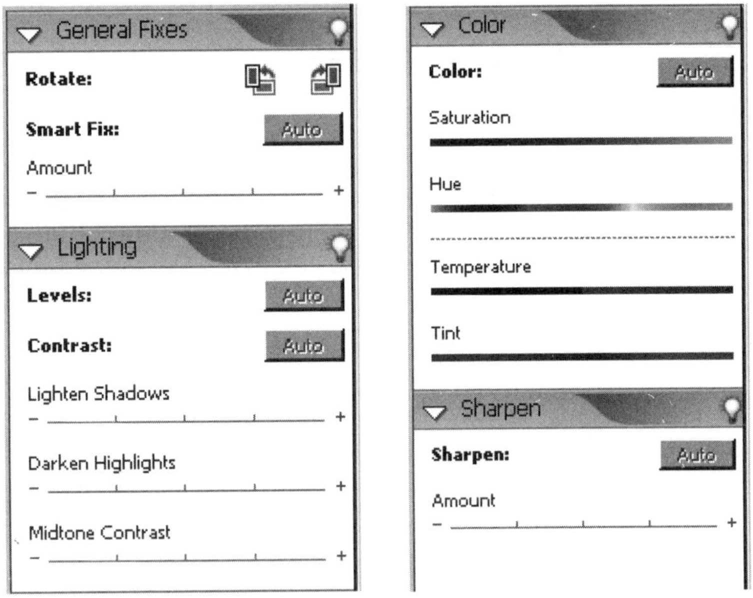

Figure 16.9 Quick Fix menu in Quick Fix mode of Elements.

You will note at the top of the menu is a one-button process called Smart Fix. Use Smart Fix for the automatic overall processing of a photograph; it does everything. Then you have one-button processing for Levels, Contrast, Color, and Sharpen. If Smart Fix doesn't work well, undo it in Edit and try one of the other Auto buttons. These can be real timesavers when they work.

Play the Percentages

When do the automatic processes work? Well, under normal circumstances they work about 70 or 80 percent of the time. We encourage you to try them. If they don't work well, go into the Enhance menu and try custom processing. Photoshop Elements is magic. Truly magic. But it can't salvage a badly taken photograph. You have to give it something to work with.

Other Functions

Here are some other functions to use:

- If a vertical photograph is horizontal, you will need to use the image editor to rotate it. Do that before you start your post-processing.

- A photograph automatically shows on your monitor in a size that makes it easy for you to view the whole thing. Use the Zoom tool to change the viewing size when you need to.

Summary

You can spend a decade learning Adobe Photoshop CS. You can spend almost as much time learning Adobe Photoshop Elements 3.0. So why just a short chapter on post-processing in this book? Adobe has made it incredibly easy for you. Don't fight it. Take advantage of it to reduce the time you spend working on your eBay photography.

If you don't need post-processing, that's great. If you need any post-processing at all, be sure to add sharpening too. There are few product photographs that can't use some sharpening.

17

Batch Processing

Batch processing is simply post-processing in Photoshop Elements 3.0 for more than one file at the same time. It can be a real time saver and is something you need to learn how to do. The first question that comes up is, When is batch processing appropriate? It's appropriate when you have taken a series of similar shots in the same lighting environment, and the shots need post-processing. It also works for resizing, which you need to do for all your photographs. Learning batch processing is an opportunity to become more efficient that you don't want to overlook.

Processing Multiple Files

Look at the Process Multiple Files panel, which you access via Edit in Elements (see Figure 17.1).

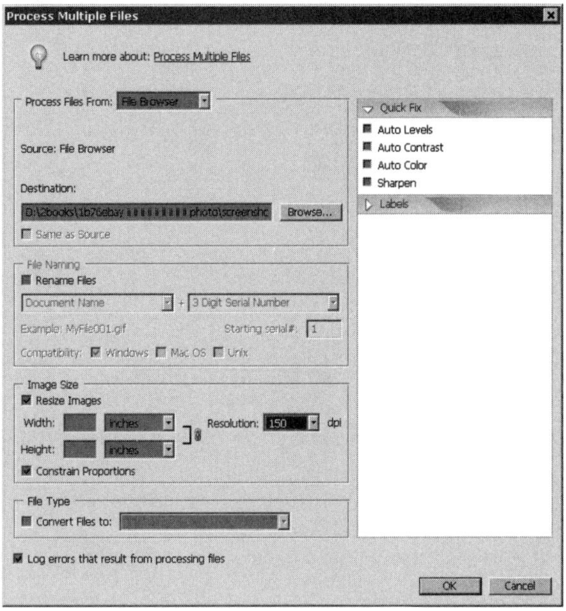

Figure 17.1 Process Multiple Files panel.

Processing

Following are the options you can employ for processing multiple files:

- Auto Levels
- Auto Contrast
- Auto Color
- Sharpen

- Resize Images

- Rename Files

- Convert Files

Remember the discussion from Chapter 16 about the automatic processing working 70 to 80 percent of the time? Well, when you do batch processing, you always need to follow up and check each photograph to make sure it turned out OK. Seven or eight out of every ten will look better. Two or three will require custom post-processing (or no post-processing). The more similar the lighting environment and the photography is for each batch that you process, the higher the processing success percentage will be.

Resize Before Sharpening

Note that with Elements in batch mode you cannot resize before sharpening as recommended in Chapter 16, unless you do your batch processing in two steps. This is unfortunate if you need sharpening. If you really need sharpening badly, however, the extra step doesn't take much more time.

Assembly

To assemble the files, move them into one folder and access that folder (see Figure 17.1 above). You also need to set a destination folder where the resulting files will reside. Alternatively, you can pick a group of individual files in the File Browser (go Edit, Browse Folders). Then go Edit, Process Multiple Files.

Get It Done

With a little planning, you can get it all done quickly and conveniently by processing files in mass. Chapter 16 shows you what you need to do. If nothing else, batch processing will enable you to conveniently resize your files. That's important to do as we have mentioned elsewhere in the book. The file renaming capability may help you with a naming system. File naming is covered in Chapter 20. The file conversion capability may be a help if your camera doesn't produce JPEG files, although that is unlikely.

Give this wonderful batch processing capability in Elements a try. You'll like it.

18

Advanced Processing

The post-processing we have outlined will get the job done for you. It's really all you need to produce clear and sharp photographs that help sell your items. And, of course, the goal is to avoid post-processing in the first place by taking photographs that don't need it. So where does that leave us with the wonderous world of post-processing, where anything is possible in a photograph? It leaves us doing a lot of work. Digital photo processing can work wonders, but advanced post-processing can also take huge amounts of time. If you decide to carry your post-processing beyond the basics, you'd better understand why you are doing so. Believe us. There are not many good business reasons for doing advanced post-processing. It's not cost-effective in most cases.

Techniques

If you want to learn some more sophisticated post-processing techniques for your product photographs, you can start by mastering an advanced image editor such as Adobe Photoshop instead of Photoshop Elements. This is a major investment of your time and energy but a necessary one for advanced post-processing. Here are some techniques:

- Create a blurred or textured background.
- Cut a product out of one photograph and paste it into another photograph that makes a better background.
- Create shadows for an item that give a more natural look.
- Use curves to fine tune instead of using levels.
- Adjust the shadows and highlights.
- Substitute colors.
- Use photo filters (simulated) to give a certain effect.
- Use RAW files generated by an expensive digital camera.
- Give an item special lighting effects (simulated).
- Create spectral highlights in all the right places (i.e., sparkle).
- Remove unsightly blemishes.
- Turn the photograph into an oil or watercolor painting (in effect).

This is just the tip of the iceberg. What you can do is unlimited. Adobe Photoshop CS is perhaps the most robust and versatile off-the-shelf software you can buy today for any human endeavor. You can spend years learning how to use it for photography, and then spend additional years learning how to use it for artwork. But then, that's not what eBay retail business is about.

Cost-Effectiveness

You really have to take a hard look at cost-effectiveness when you get into advanced post-processing. For instance, Joe sold an Olympus OM-4 film camera with four lenses on eBay in 2003 that he had owned for 18 years. After he photographed the camera and lens in a one-hour session with a 3-MP Canon A70, he spent another hour tweaking the photographs in Adobe Photoshop (see Photo 77). He sold the camera and lenses (camera set) for over $2,000. Was the post-processing worth his time and effort?

Let's say his time is worth $35 per hour. Two hours of photographic work then costs $70. He expected to sell the camera set for about $1,000. Instead, he sold it for over $2,000. He thinks the photographs helped sell the set for the higher price. The $70 doesn't look like a huge expense under the circumstances, so it appears as though Joe's time was well spent. But then, Joe wasn't in business. He was just an amateur photographer selling some old camera equipment.

Suppose instead that a camera dealer sells the same equipment with a $500 margin. That is, her gross profit on the sale is $500. Now to determine her net profit on the sale, she has to assign a portion of her overhead to the sale in addition to any expenses incurred in selling the camera set. In making these calculations, the $70 of time for photography starts to look like a huge expense.

The fact is that the camera set could have been photographed in half the time, and the photographs could have been used without post-processing. Therefore, the cost would have been $17.50 instead of $70. That makes a lot more sense for an item with $500 in gross profit. The question you have to ask is, How much did the post-processing contribute to the higher sale price? That's a question that's hard to answer, but if you ask the question, at least you're taking a realistic approach to cost-effectiveness.

So let's conclude here by saying that if the cost-effectiveness of post-processing is doubtful in the case of the camera example above, it isn't in the following two cases. First, post-processing is not cost-effective when you attempt to sell an item with low gross profit (i.e., somewhere below $500). For example, suppose you sell a tool set for $400 with a gross profit margin of $150. A $70 expense for photography is much too much.

Second, as the gross profit goes up (i.e., from $500) for an item, the likelihood of post-processing being cost-effective also goes up. For instance, $70 for photography doesn't seem like much when you sell a car for $12,000.

In other words, don't waste your time with post-processing unless an item has a high gross profit. You don't have to be a genius to figure that out. What you do have to figure out for yourself, however, is exactly where that line is between what is cost-effective and what is not. Is it at $500 of gross profit? $200 of gross profit? Or $800 of gross profit? It's your call.

One Last Technique

Now that you have a proper and practical persepctive on photographic post-processing, let us cover one last technique: Lightening shadows and darkening highlights. This is a fabulous technique for general photography and may be one you can use occasionally to either enhance a photograph you've taken or to save yourself the hassle of having to rephotograph an item. This capability is new to both Photoshop CS and Photoshop Elements 3.0.

Let's revisit the Milk-Bone photograph (see Photo 68). The shape of the metal box creates a shadow in the front, even with a light beaming at it from each side. In Elements go Enhance, Adjust Lighting, Shadows/Highlights (see Figure 18.1).

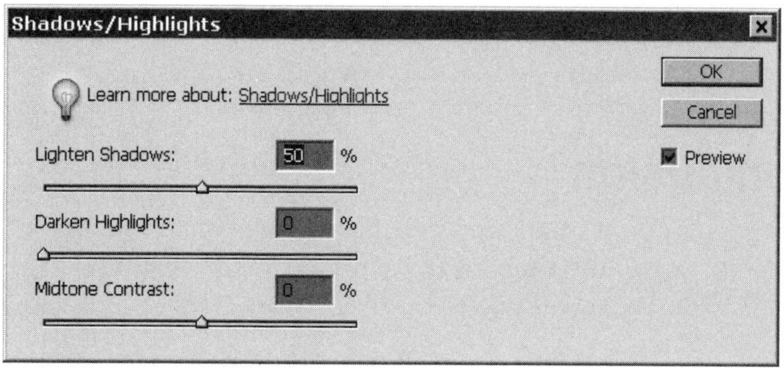

Figure 18.1 Shadows/Highlights panel in Photoshop Elements 3.0.

For the Milk-Bone photograph, Joe lightened the shadows 50 percent and darkened the highlights 10 percent. (He also added one-button Levels and custom adjustment of Brightness/Contrast.) The result is a photograph that's more evenly lighted (see Photo 69). This is a slick trick. It emulates an old darkroom technique that not only took hours to complete but could only be done by an accomplished photographer. In Elements, it's quite easy.

Another photograph that has a more subtle shadow in the front is the hat in Photo 70. Lightening the shadows 50 percent takes away much of the front shadow in this underexposed shot and makes the details of the hat easier to inspect (see Photo 71). Notice that this process also lightens up the entire photograph, a task that you would need to do another way if you didn't use the Shadows/Highlights function.

It's Included

Another way to adjust shadows and highlights is in the Elements Quick Fix mode. Under Contrast, you can move sliders to adjust shadows and highlights. Unfortunately, it's difficult to work precisely with sliders because you don't get a percentage number as you do in the Enhance mode. Nonetheless, you can do a quick fix visually.

Note that Smart Fix actually includes adjusting shadows and highlights automatically. What a fabulous deal!

Conclusion

Advanced post-processing is great—not to mention fun—if you can spare the time away from your other business tasks. When you do, make sure it's cost-effective.

VI

Using Your Photographs

19

Storing Photos on the Web

To publish photographs on the Web for everyone to see, you must place them someplace on the Web. Like any webpage or Web media, they must each have a unique Internet address; that is, a unique URL. There are many places where you can store your photographs on the Web. eBay will even do it for you. But like everything else in business, you will want to store them in the place that is the most cost-effective. Therefore, with cost-effectiveness in mind, this chapter will look at each potential place where you can store your photographs on the Web.

Photo Websites

There are a large number of websites that enable you to store your photographs. At some of them, you can store your photographs for free. At others, you will have to a pay a nominal or even a substantial monthly fee to store your photographs. In addition to storing your photographs, a lot of websites have features that enable you to do other things with your photographs. For instance, you might be able to look at them in an album (catalog), use an online image editor to edit them, or otherwise manage them. Each website that offers such services bears investigation so that you can find something that matches your work style. As you'll read in Chapter 20, you will want to be able to use your naming system to make sense of your photographs wherever you store them on the Web or offline.

eBay

For each of your auctions you can store one photograph on eBay for free but only for the duration of the auction. Thereafter, eBay deletes it. For each additional photograph that you add to your auction ad, eBay will charge you a small fee (currently 15 cents). Although this sounds like a good deal, it's not going to work very well if you sell your products on an independent website, do datafeed marketing (see Chapter 21), or otherwise need your photographs for ecommerce other than eBay. So our recommendation is to forego using eBay as the place where you store your digital photographs online.

Host ISP

If you have an independent website, you are probably using a host Internet service provider (ISP) to provide a place for your webpages to be reached on the Web. In other words, the host ISP hosts your website by providing a place to put your webpages where people browsing the Web can find them. Each webpage has a unique URL. A webpage is simply a plain text file with plain text markups that create the typesetting and layout for the text page. The markup language is called hypertext markup language (HTML), and consequently we call the plain text file an HTML file. The point here is that if you can place an HTML file at a place on the Web furnished by your host ISP, you can certainly put an image file (digital photograph) there too. Indeed, if you have an independent website, your website space at your host ISP is an ideal place to put your digital photograph files. By placing them there, each will have a unique URL on the Web, and it won't cost you anything additional to store them there.

Dial-Up ISP

Your dial-up ISP is different from your host ISP in that your dial-up ISP furnishes you with a connection to the Internet for your own computer. In our definition of dial-up ISP, we also include ISPs that provide DSL broadband service, cable broadband service, or satellite broadband service. Whether dial-up, DSL, cable, or satellite, you have to have a connection to the Internet to get online and browse the Web.

Your dial-up ISP must also furnish you with space online, because dial-up ISPs invariably provide email service. There must be someplace to store your incoming email until such time as you choose to access it, download it, or read it. Consequently, dial-up ISPs more often than not also act as host ISPs. That is, they will provide you space to put up webpages. This space is usually provided free along with your dial-up service. You can use this space to put up a website (a collection of webpages). And as we know, if you can do that, you can also use that space to store your digital photographs on the Web at no additional cost.

What's the difference between a host ISP and a dial-up ISP when it comes to actually hosting webpages? Well, a host ISP usually provides a lot more space for your website and in addition often provides a lot more services that webmasters need to operate their websites. In contrast, a dial-up ISP usually just provides a comparatively small amount of space and little else. Nonetheless, the space that your dial-up ISP provides is just as good as the space that your host ISP provides, even though it may not be as much space. The good news is that if you run out of space with your dial-up ISP to store your digital photographs on the Web, you may be able to purchase additional space for a small monthly fee.

Hence, the message of this section is don't overlook your dial-up ISP as a place to upload your digital photographs for placement on the Web. Once they're on the Web, they can be pulled in to your eBay auction ad quite easily.

Auction Management Service

If you subscribe to an auction management service, as you should to manage your eBay retail business, such a service usually provides a place for you to store your digital photographs on the Web. There is usually a nominal monthly fee if, in fact, the auction management services charges you anything additional for it. This is probably the best place for your digital photographs because the auction management service may have some convenient method of placing them in your auction ads when you store them with the auction management service. Consequently, when you choose an auction management service, you may want to examine what storage it will provide for digital photographs on the Web, how much it will cost, and what kind of convenience it will provide.

Conclusion

In order to use your digital photographs in your auction ads, you have to put them someplace on the Web. Where you place them is a matter of cost and convenience. Evaluate the alternatives and pick one that suits your work style and your pocketbook.

20

Building an Archive

The photographs you take can add up quickly. For instance, let's say that you take three photographs a day for every working day of a 50-week year (this assumes you take a two-week vacation). That's 250 days of photography resulting in 750 photographs just in one year. If you take 30 photographs each day instead, that's 7,500 photographs a year. More than one version of each (see Photos 74 and 75) adds even more. Clearly you must develop a strategy about how you are going to account for and keep track of all of these photographs. You must design an archive for storing photographs that makes sense to you.

In this chapter, we're not going to tell you exactly what to do. Rather, we're going to identify some issues for you to consider in setting up your own system with the software that you pick. Finally, in Appendix III we provide you with a list of potential programs that you can evaluate before you set up your archival system.

The Directory

You need to use the file (folder) directory in your operating system to set up a framework to store your photographs (see Figure 20.1).

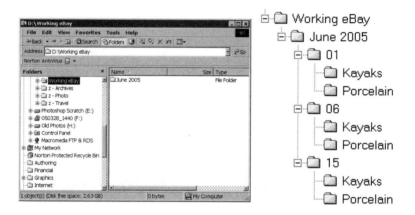

Figure 20.1 Left: Windows Explorer, the file (folder) directory in Windows. Right: eBay directory as described in this section.

The directory is hierarchical. For example, you might have a folder named June. In that folder will go all the photographs that you take in June. Since you take a lot of photographs each day, however, under the June folder you may want to have additional folders for each workday of the month. Let's call these subfolders.

Your first subfolder will be entitled *01*. That stands for June 1. Thus, for every day during June that you take photographs, you will have a corresponding subfolder labeled with a two-digit number. Suppose you sell porcelain on eBay, and your husband sells inflatable kayaks.

You both use the same computer, software, and systems for your selling. Consequently, under the subfolder 01 you may want to create two more subfolders. (You might call these sub-subfolders, but you get the idea.) One of these subfolders will be named *Porcelain* and the other *Kayaks*. The photographs you take for your porcelain will be stored in the *Porcelain* subfolder, and the photographs your husband takes of the inflatable kayaks and equipment will be stored in the *Kayaks* subfolder.

This example is presented here just to remind you how the file directory system in your operating system works. If you can't use the file directory system in your operating system, you will need to take some time to learn it. Otherwise, you may find yourself at a disadvantage when you try to build an archival system for your product photographs. Nonetheless, this is not to say you must use the file directory as an archival system for storing your photographs, although that is certainly one workable alternative.

Use the Numbers

Your digital camera will label digital photographs, which are digital files. Each file will be labeled with a sequential number. This enables you to identify each file (photograph) by its unique file name; that is, the number that the digital camera assigns to the file.

Why not use this system to your own advantage? The file names are unique, and the camera provides them automatically. There's no reason to impose a system that replaces the good work your camera already does.

These sequential numbers by themselves are not enough to do the job for you. But used together with the file directory system in your operating system and a photo archive program, the numbers should prove valuable. Keep in mind, there is nothing to prevent you from adding on to these numbers. For instance, suppose you take a photograph of a dinner place setting of the china you are selling. The pattern is named Morning Glory. The photograph file name assigned by the camera is EIC001359.jpg. You can add something to that file name without replacing the number. For instance, before the period preceding the file extension (here, the file extension is jpg) you can add a hyphen and insert DinnerPlate and MorningGlory. Now the file name reads EIC001359-DinnerPlate-MorningGlory.jpg.

One great advantage of using the numbers is that a photograph file name always has a unique name (i.e., the unique number). If you misplace the file in the wrong folder, it won't accidently have the same name as any other number in that folder.

Again, we're not advocating that you create this type of a system. This is just an example of what you might find expedient. The system that you create should be one that enables you to find photographs that you need quickly and easily in the archive. Thus, doing an add-on rather than replacement is one strategy that you can use.

Set the Camera

If you are going to use the camera to provide unique numbers for file names, you need to set the camera to do so. Otherwise, the camera may go back to number 1 each time you delete the photographs from the memory card.

Information Names

As you've already seen in the prior section, identifying information in a file name is often very handy. What are some of the things you might want to include in a file name in order to more easily identify the file and to more easily find what you're looking for when you search your archives for photographs that you need?

Here are two of the things that we have found to be handy:

Date Dates can be very handy in helping you remember where to find something. Putting a date in the name is one strategy that can make it easy to use a photo archive. We express the dates using six digits. The first two digits are the year, the second two digits are the month, and the last two digits are the day. If you express your dates this way, they will automatically organize the files sequentially in time. Any other way will not achieve that purpose. Thus, 050306 is March 6, 2005. And 061023 is October 23, 2006. We find that these dates in the name of a file can be useful, but we do not automatically recommend them to you, because you need to decide what will be the most useful for your purposes.

Description Naturally, the description of the item photographed makes a useful file name. What we recommend here is that you do not economize with your description. Do not use abbreviations that you will not understand a year or five years from now. Do not leave out anything that you need to absolutely identify the item. In the example that we used in the prior section, the item was almost absolutely identified. In the set of china, there is only one dinner plate, and the manufacturer of the china uses only one unique name to identify a specific place setting. The only thing left out of this description is the manufacturer's brand name (e.g., Noritake). In this case, it might make sense to go back and add Noritake to the name of the file.

Sequential Labeling

We strongly recommend that you archive the original file for each photograph from your digital camera unaltered. Consequently, the first thing you should do with any post-processing is to make a copy with which you will do your post-processing work. We have found it expedient to give that copy a different and unique name from the original file created by your digital camera.

For instance, suppose the name of the file provided by your digital camera is EIC001359.jpg. One way to identify the working copy is to simply add a hyphen and a lowercase letter b. Or just add a lowercase b without the hyphen. This identical file can be stored either in the same folder as the original or in a separate working folder. We recommend a separate working folder.

Let's say you run it through a batch process as explained in Chapter 17. The result of the batch processing is that you should have improved digital photographs. You might want to save these files with a hyphen and the letter c or just the letter c without the hyphen. Again, you can store these in the same folder as the previous files or in a separate folder. Now, when you look at all your photograph files, you can tell which ones are the camera originals, which ones are the work copies, and which ones are the processed copies. The ones you will use for your eBay ad are the ones labeled c. The batch processing capability in image editors often includes the capability to rename files (i.e., the batch processing can add the c automatically).

Suppose the batch processing did not work on a particular photograph, and you want to do some custom processing. When you get done with your custom processing you might want to label the resulting file with the letter d with or without a hyphen. That will indicate that the batch processing did not work well and it required custom post-processing to create a usable photograph.

Examples:

EIC001359.jpg	Original
EIC001359-b.jpg	Working copy
EIC001359-c.jpg	Processed copy
EIC001359-d.jpg	Custom processed copy

Software

There are plenty of photo archive programs around (photo albums, photo catalogs, etc.). Photoshop Elements 3.0 comes with one. Adobe sells another one called Adobe Photo Album. There are dozens of these programs available. Your first task is to pick one with which you feel comfortable (i.e., one which you find easy to use). Once you've picked a program, you need to learn to use it in such a way that it makes sense to you. That means you'll need to dig into the manual and practice what you learn until you can run the program well.

It is confusing to evaluate photo archive software. If you develop your own archive system using the file directory, you need an archive program only to view your files and to supply some convenient ancillary functions. Essentially all photo archive programs will do that for you. If you want software that provides a ready-made archive system for you, then you need to try a variety of programs to determine which one best fits your work style and idea of how to store and keep track of your photographs.

Uploading

From your archive, you will need to upload your photographs to the place on the Web you have chosen to make them available (see Chapter 19). Some archive programs have the built-in capability to do this for you. If you can use an archive program or image editor to do this for you, that's great. Do it.

We recommend, however, that you consider using an FTP program such as the Ipswitch WS_FTP (*http://ipswitch.com*) to upload your images to the Web. It might be easier than using an archive program or image editor, and it will likely provide more functionality and flexibility. Then too, you will be able to continue to use it knowledgeably even if you switch image editors or archive programs.

Conclusion

If we provided you with a file labeling system and filing system, you probably wouldn't like them. Dream up something yourself that fits your needs. Make sure that it creates unique file names. Make sure it organizes your files. Make sure the system is expandable. You never know how many photographs the future will bring as your business thrives. Use an archive viewer to look at your files.

The alternative is to use a photo archive program to label and organize your photographs. Read the software instruction manual carefully to determine how you can take full advantage of the software to make your job as an eBay photographer easier and more efficient.

21

Marketing and Copyrights

Datafeed marketing is a new concept that enables you to expand the marketplaces for your products at little additional effort or cost to you. The idea is that you keep all the data on your products in the database on your desktop. You export that data to eBay auctions and eBay Stores in order to fill webpage templates with information. The templates thereby become the listing pages in the auctions and the catalog pages in Stores. If you can export the data to eBay auctions and eBay Stores to create listing pages (catalog pages), you can also export the data to other online marketplaces to create catalog entries.

This relatively new concept of datafeed marketing is a very cost-effective way to boost your sales. Read Joe's book *Building Your eBay Traffic the Smart Way* to learn more about this exciting ecommerce technique.

In this book, however, we are only concerned with how to handle the digital photographs that must accompany the text in any catalog entries or pages for any marketplace. With that in mind, there are a number of considerations to keep in mind when building a system for digital photographs that will accommodate all marketplaces.

Where?

If you are going to sell in other marketplaces besides eBay auctions and eBay Stores, you need to store your product photographs in some independent location on the Web. Obviously, uploading your photographs to eBay will not make them available to other marketplaces. As we discussed in Chapter 19, you have numerous options as to where to store your photographs on the Web. You will want to pick an option that makes the photographs available to any website that hosts your product catalog entries or pages.

Size and Download Time

As we've discussed before, large photographs take a longer time to download thereby inconveniencing prospective buyers. Consequently, you want to keep your photographs as large as possible for easy viewing but as small as possible for quick downloading. We have recommended a typical size of 400 × 300 pixels for eBay photographs. That's large enough to see easily but small enough to download in a reasonable time.

Unfortunately, the eBay size that we recommend is not allowed in many other online marketplaces to which you may decide to export your data to create catalog entries. The result will be that the HTML pages for those marketplaces will reduce the size of your photograph to their standard size, but the photograph will remain the same size for downloading purposes. Thus, you get a smaller photograph without the convenience to perspective buyers of a shorter download time. This is something you will want to avoid, and it's worth taking a little time to set up a photograph system that will take this into account.

If you look at the size of the eBay photograph that appears at the top of every eBay listing web page, you may come to the conclusion that this is a good size to use for your primary photograph for all catalog entries or pages. It's not a very big size, but it will download very quickly for eBay because eBay will not have to resize it. In addition, keeping your first photograph smaller does not prevent you from including additional photographs in your eBay auction and eBay Store catalog at the size that we recommend.

Now when you export your datafeed to another marketplace such as Froogle, which has a smaller standard photograph size than eBay, you will not be sending such a large photograph to be downloaded. The Froogle catalog will still make your photograph smaller than it appears on eBay, but it will be starting with a smaller photograph and a quicker download time.

What Is the Guideline?

What is the guideline to be derived from the consideration of using datafeed marketing? The guideline is simply to decide which of your marketplaces requires the largest photograph for a primary catalog photograph, and use that as the size for your primary (first) photograph.

Because most marketplaces use small photographs, the largest size you'll have to use anywhere is likely still to be small. Therefore, your primary photograph should be a size that fits this guideline. Because most marketplaces do not allow additional photographs (i.e., a second or third photograph), your additional photographs for eBay are irrelevant to datafeed marketing. When you use additional photographs on eBay, you should make them the size that we have recommended (i.e., 400 × 300 pixels).

Quality

Based on the discussion above, you can understand that the primary photograph is the most important one. It should be the photograph that best displays your item for inspection. In many marketplaces other than eBay, you only get one chance to show the item. So the characteristic you are looking for in that one photograph is not necessarily the most attractive photograph but the photograph that best displays the item for sale.

Multiple Photographs

Because you can do anything you want to in the description portion of an eBay listing webpage, you can include as many photographs of the item for sale as you desire. Multiple photographs are very desirable, particularly for expensive items; they really help make a sale. The question then becomes, How do I use additional photographs in Web marketplaces that only accept one photograph? That depends on what kind of ecommerce system you have set up for your eBay business. If you are using your eBay Store as your ecommerce website, then all click-throughs in your catalog entries or pages in any other marketplace will come back to your eBay Store catalog. If you have additional photographs in your eBay Store pages, perspective buyers will see them there.

If you have an ecommerce website with catalog pages, a click through in another marketplace will take prospective buyers to that catalog page. That's where you will need to display your additional photographs.

Each marketplace is different, and there are more coming online. There is certainly a lot of innovation now in the ecommerce industry. So you can expect that some of the marketplaces will eventually have catalog entries that will accommodate your additional photographs. You will have to evaluate each marketplace to see what you can do in the way of including extra photographs. The optimal size is still 400 × 300 pixels in any online marketplace, so any additional photographs beyond the first one will certainly be appropriate for every marketplace that will accept them.

Copyrights

If you use manufacturers' photographs, you have exactly the same problem for datafeed marketing as you do with your own photographs. You just obtain the photographs from a different source: from the manufacturer instead from your studio. Consequently, all considerations covered by this chapter apply to manufacturers' photographs too.

There is an additional consideration here, however, that has little to do with photographic techniques. It can be identified by the question, Do you have permission to use a manufacturer's photograph? It is likely to be a copyright violation to use a manufacturer's photograph without permission. Yet certainly on eBay and also in other online marketplaces, many online retailers use manufacturers' photographs to promote sales.

For eBay auctions, it's not so risky. After all, the photograph only stays up for the length of the auction, which is ten days at most. However, in an eBay Store, the product can be for sale for a much longer time. In that situation, it's much more likely to be discovered by the manufacturer or possibly by eBay, and you may find yourself in a bit of trouble over it. Likewise, in other marketplaces where your item remains for sale over a long period, your use of a manufacturer's photograph is more likely to be discovered by either the manufacturer or the owner of the marketplace. Again, you might find yourself in a bit of trouble over it. The best practice is to use manufacturers' photographs only with permission.

If, however, you are an official dealer of the products you sell, you have an implied right to use photographs of the products taken by the manufacturer to promote sales. In such a case, you shouldn't worry about copyright violations.

Watermarks

Many online retailers watermark their photographs. You don't want to borrow one of these photographs for your own retail business. An irate competitor might come after you. However, the real question is, Should you watermark your photographs to make it unlikely that your competitors will use them?

There are two reasons to use watermarks in your product photographs. First, the watermark identifies your retail name or company. Should somebody steal the photograph, they will advertise your business. Second, the watermark tends to keep other retailers from stealing your photographs to sell identical products in competition with your retail business.

Unfortunately, there's a fallacy here. The only place you can put your watermark where it won't interfere with your great photograph is along one of the edges of the photograph. Whether it's left-hand or right-hand or top or bottom edge, a competitor can easily crop out your watermark to steal and effectively use your photograph. On the other hand, if you put your watermark across the photograph where it cannot be cropped out, you will severely impair the photograph and thereby diminish your sales effort. We do not recommend that you put watermarks anywhere except along an edge of your photographs.

Perhaps a more effective way of handling your competitors when they steal your photographs is to write them a nasty email letting them know that you know they have done so. Although the first paragraph of that email should be custom written to handle the situation, you can use a boilerplate paragraph as the second paragraph of that email. Find a nasty paragraph that threatens legal action under the copyright statutes if the offender doesn't cease and desist from using the copyrighted photograph and use it as the boilerplate.

In order to make this threat credible, you have to make a copyright notice part of your watermark while keeping in mind that you are going to put the watermark at the edge of the photograph.

The first part of the copyright notice is the copyright sign © or *(c)*. The second part, which immediately follows, is the year. The third part which follows after a space after the year is the holder of the copyright. That might be your name or the name of your company. If nothing follows, that's enough.

To make this copyright notice effective in some other countries, however, you will have to put a period after the name of the copyright holder and then a space. That space must be followed by the phrase "All rights reserved" followed by a period.

©2005 Elegant Clocks, Inc. All rights reserved.

That makes for a long copyright notice. Since these are just product pictures and not exotic works of art that you have spent weeks and weeks working on, we recommend that you leave off the additional phrase. See Photo 76 right-hand side.

In addition, we recommend that you copyright your product photographs in the name of your company rather than in your own name so that they have an advertising effect. Read *Building Your eBay Traffic the Smart Way* for the advertising considerations in regard to naming your retail company so that your company promotes your retail business.

Copyright Statutes

The copyright statutes make it easier to sue someone for infringement and collect if the copyright is registered than if you did not register the copyright. However, whether you register it or not you still have a copyright on photographs that you create.

Again, let us state emphatically: Do not use watermarks across your product photographs. There's no point in taking great photographs to generate great sales and then defacing the photographs so they are not effective. Yeah, yeah, we know, you see it all over the Web. But that doesn't mean it's smart. This is not some fashionable game you're playing so that you can brag about being a cool ecommerce retailer. This is about making sales, which means making it easy for your prospective buyers to make a purchase decision. A photograph with a watermark across the middle just doesn't cut it. And if the watermark does not include a copyright notification, it is not as meaningful legally.

How to Make a Watermark

Use the text tool in Photoshop Elements 3.0, Standard Edit mode. Type the copyright notice in a color that contrasts with the photograph but doesn't overwhelm it. Normally a watermark is very faint. In this case, you want people to be able to read it. Move the text to an appropriate edge of the photograph.

Summary

Set up a system for the primary photograph for each product so that you can use it intelligently for any other online marketplace.

As you promulgate your retail products on eBay and to other marketplaces, you want to use effective photographs but ones that are identified as yours. You don't want competitors to steal the photographs from you. The best way to do this is to put a copyright notice along one edge of the photograph.

VII

Strategies for Increasing Profits

22

Planning

Planning your eBay photography has to do with focusing on the important elements of your eBay photographic operation. The guiding beacon is cost-effectiveness. Remember that cost-effectiveness takes into account both your time (which is valuable), your effort (which should be rewarded), and your money.

Sure, you can drift into your eBay photography, running after this piece of equipment or that whenever you need it, searching around the house for household items that can be used for props, and setting up a makeshift studio whenever you need it. Yet that would result in inefficiency—an unnecessary waste of your time, effort, and perhaps even money. Thus, the theme of this chapter is getting organized for cost-effectiveness.

Studio

You need to pick a spot for your studio in your home. As mentioned before, a 7 × 7 foot space with a table is the minimum you'll need. Anything less and your efficiency will be compromised. For general product photography, the space must accommodate a table, background paper, and several photo lights and stands. And don't forget a tripod and a place for you to sit.

If you don't have the space to spare in your home, you'll need to think through how to create such a space temporarily. Perhaps you can use a folding table. Perhaps you can buy studio equipment that can be easily put away and taken out as you need it. In other words, plan a temporary studio that you can take out and set up as you need it and then put away. Being able to do so efficiently, though, takes some thought and planning.

Another consideration for your studio is lighting. There are three issues here. First, you need to have adequate light to work when the photo lights are not turned on to shoot photographs. Second, if you use your computer in this same space, you will want to make sure there are no lights that reflect off the screen of your computer so as to make the screen difficult to read.

Third, if you have a window nearby your studio, you need to use some kind of window treatment to control the daylight. Either you will set up your studio to use the daylight, which means orienting your studio to take advantage of the window, or you will need to put a shade over the window to control the light so it does not interfere with your photography. Of course, if you do your photographic work at night, the window is not necessarily a problem except perhaps during the long days of summer.

Equipment

Purchase and organize your equipment so that your studio becomes an easy place to work. Go on a shopping spree to buy everything that you need. The easiest way to use your equipment, of course, is to leave it set up so that you can walk into your studio and start shooting.

Keep in mind that your studio is a part of your eBay retail business, and as such, you should treat it like any other business environment. You need to take a professional approach to creating a good work environment. If you don't, it's your own time, effort, and money that you will be wasting.

Workflow

Setting up workflow is analogous to setting up an assembly line. For the photography part of your workflow, for instance, you will need a staging area for your items to be photographed. Then the items need to be taken one by one to be photographed. You need to have another staging area where they are placed after the photographs are completed. Staging areas might be on the same table that you use for your studio, but wherever they are, they need to be someplace to ensure a smooth workflow.

Organize your items into groups that can be shot the same way (e.g., small items, tabletop items, etc.). Taking photographs randomly may necessitate a lot of extra setting up and equipment moving. So stage your photographs so that you can do similar shots at the same time with the same setup. Likewise, schedule your outdoor photographs all at the same time rather than mixing them together with your studio photographs.

Integrate your post-processing into the photography assembly line. Complete your shooting and then move on to do your post-processing. An important part of planning for post-processing is deciding exactly what you need to do to each photograph, exactly what you will name each photo file, and exactly how you will achieve the files. In addition, whenever possible, you need to use batch processing functions in post-processing to ensure efficiency. All of these are discussed in earlier chapters.

Our recommendation is that you do your post-processing somewhere outside your studio. This is natural because your computer is likely to be in your office rather than your studio, and that's a good place to do your post-processing. Until you have planned, experimented with, and smoothed out your workflow, however, you might want to do your post-processing in your studio temporarily. That will make it handy to go back and reshoot certain items. Once you figure out a good workflow, though, it should be a rare occasion when you need to go back to reshoot an item.

For systems that use a computer as part of the studio workflow equipment, such as the Photosimile 200 (see Chapter 6), the computer occupies an important place in the studio. These types of comprehensive systems can be very efficient and are certainly worth your consideration. However, you need to factor their relatively high cost into your cost-effectiveness calculations.

Summary

Planning takes some effort up front but can save you time, effort, and money. Hey, you're in the eBay retail business. You don't want to spend any more time taking photographs than you have to.

23

Enhanced Product Photography

In Chapter 13, we cover situations in which you need to do something more than straightforward product photography. One situation is where the item itself has aesthetic appeal as one of its primary characteristics. Jewelry is a good example. Such items are sometimes best displayed with a background that is more than just plain white or grey seamless background paper. And we recommend you consider using props to display such items more attractively, such as a black velvet display for jewelry.

A basic premise of the book is that you do not have time to do an attractive advertising setup for each item that you photograph. Another premise of the book is that you do not have the knowledge and background needed for doing such presentations well. Although we think we do a pretty good job of covering product photography well, we do not claim to have the advertising and artistic knowledge and background to teach you how to make good advertising displays for your products. Nonetheless, we have some tips for how you can handle situations which require advertising displays to maximize sales prices.

Thus the first point of discussion is, How do you tell when you need an advertising display? The second is, How do you set up and make an advertising display without being an advertising expert or an artist?

When Do You Need an Advertising Display?

Doing an advertising display for a product is only justified when it is cost-effective. Clearly for a low-priced item that may give you a profit of $5 to $50, making an advertising display to generate a few extra bucks from the auction is probably not worth your time and effort.

Big ticket items are different. If you stand to make a profit of $200 to $1,500 or more, it might be worth your time and effort to create a nice appealing setting in which to display your item before you photograph it. The decision that you have to make is, What is your time worth? How much profit are you likely to make? How much more profit are you likely to make if you put the item in an attractive setting to photograph it?

Once you answer these questions, you can determine not only when it's worth it to go to the trouble of creating an advertising setting but also exactly how much time you can afford to spend on creating that setting.

These calculations, of course, are personal to everyone. We cannot provide you with a set formula to figure this out. Keep in mind, though, that the better you become at taking studio photographs, the more cost-effectively you can do something extra for big ticket items.

Another situation for which you can justify creating an advertising display for an item is when you sell the item over and over again and use the photographs over and over again. This, of course, is a situation where you buy certain items at wholesale and sell them at retail on an ongoing basis. Indeed, creating an advertising display for your photographs is particularly appropriate for new merchandise that you sell continuously. Keep in mind, for new merchandise, you don't have to show any defects in the product. The product is assumed to be in perfect condition. By taking a modestly expensive item and selling it over and over again, you are in effect turning it into a big ticket item that justifies spending more time on its product photography.

Creating an Advertising Display

It's actually quite easy to create an advertising display. You don't have to have advertising knowledge or background, and you don't have to be an artist. You simply have to be a copycat. What we recommend that you do to create an advertising display is to go look in places where identical or similar items are advertised.

Such places might be newspapers (especially advertising inserts), magazines, television commercials, product literature, catalogs, and so forth. Use what you find in such advertising; that is, simply look around the house to see what you have that you can use to create a similar advertising display for your product. For example, suppose you sell crystal water glasses. Simply go to the Sunday newspaper advertising supplement to find a department store ad that features similar glasses. Take the ideas from the advertising display and use them together with things you have around the house. That will give you the basis to put together a similar advertising display.

The crystal water glasses are likely to be found in a photograph which shows them with place settings on a table. That should be easy for you to copy. Photograph the crystal glasses on your own dining table with your own place settings.

Always stay focused on what you're trying to do. In this case you're trying to create an advertising setting with the least amount of time, effort, and expense that will sell your product. And you do it by copying the work of professionals. You're not trying to win an international advertising award. Consequently, there will be plenty of polished advertising that it does not make sense to copy or imitate. It would be too time-consuming and likely not cost-effective.

Remember the example from Chapter 1 where the advertising director arranged to photograph the waffle iron using an attractive woman in a white evening gown (with the flowers and white background)? If you tried to emulate such an advertising setup for a waffle iron that you were selling, that particular approach to advertising would probably be much more trouble than it's worth. You would have to find a model, buy flowers, and provide a very large white background in order to make that advertising project work. And any time you have a person in the photograph, it makes the photography even more difficult. It would be smarter to copy a more domestic setting for advertising a waffle iron, and a domestic setting would be much easier to copy.

Be a Copycat

Why do we recommend that you be a copycat? First, you have nothing to lose by being a copycat. You are unlikely to copy the advertising setup exactly—just the idea, which is not copyrightable—and any potential copyright therefore becomes a moot consideration. Second, the advertising industry has spent billions and billions of dollars attempting to figure out what appeals to consumers. Their findings are reflected in the advertising that we see everyday, the very kind that we recommend that you copy. Why reinvent the wheel? Why not take advantage of all those billions of dollars of research? Keep it simple. Keep it easy. Just be a copycat.

Post-Processing

In addition to taking the time and energy to provide an advertising setting for certain of your items, it makes sense also to spend extra time editing the images. Again, it's all a matter of cost-effectiveness. Image editing is one of the most time consuming tasks in the history of mankind. It's very easy to get carried away with it. You just feel compelled to get that photograph perfect. And image editing software enables you to do so. But not without a lot of work!

So again, apply your cost-effectiveness calculations to determine exactly how much time you can spend editing your advertising photographs to get the attractive effect that you desire. Certainly, you can spend more time editing big ticket or repeat sale photographs than individual items for sale. The question is, How much more time?

Inspection

Even when you create an advertising photograph, it must still serve the primary purpose of eBay photographs. It must enable prospective buyers to inspect the item. If the advertising photograph doesn't do that, then you have failed in your primary mission, which is to provide buyers with the visual inspection online that substitutes for a physical inspection in a physical retail store.

When all is confusing and undecided, you can't go wrong providing a standard studio photograph that displays an item well for inspection. Adding an advertising enhancement is just an optional process, which might increase sales if the primary mission is accomplished. Don't lose sight of your primary mission for your eBay photography or your sales are more likely to decrease than increase due to your advertising photographs.

Summary

Yes, an advertising display is appropriate for certain items and for certain situations. A measure of what you can do intelligently to accommodate these situations is dictated by cost-effectiveness. You don't have to be an advertiser or an artist to do a good job, but you do have to be realistic about the time and effort you can allocate to doing advertising photography.

Epilogue

As an eBay seller or retailer, you need to learn to do your photography well to maximize your sales on eBay and save time. This book will help you do that.

Of course, there's always more to learn. Fortunately, there are many books on digital photography and post-processing that you will find useful. A general digital photography background will help you with your eBay product photography. And we recommend that you learn more about photography as your time permits. After all, you can use it for your family too.

Beyond eBay photography, there are more things to learn to make your eBay retail business as profitable as possible. Joe has written four more books you will find helpful. The first is *eBay the Smart Way, Fourth Edition*. This book covers the basics for both buyers and sellers, and you will need to read this before you read Joe's other eBay books, if you're not already a seasoned eBay veteran.

The second is *eBay Business the Smart Way, Second Edition*. This is a basic book on starting an eBay retail business and will save you a lot of time and effort, if your eBay retail business is still in its start-up phase.

The third is *eBay Global the Smart Way*. It shows how to increase your sales significantly and inexpensively by simply accepting orders from buyers living abroad. It also provides information on importing products to sell.

The fourth is *Building Your eBay Traffic the Smart Way*. It shows you how to do datafeed marketing, an easy and inexpensive way to substantially increase your sales by selling on Froogle and other online marketplaces. It also covers other leading online marketing techniques including Joe's opinion as to the cost-effectiveness of each.

Another eBay book Joe has written is *eBay Motors the Smart Way*. It may not help you with your eBay business, but it will help you get a good deal for yourself when you buy or sell a vehicle.

Whether you're an eBay seller or retailer, we wish you the best of luck on eBay. And should you discover a new eBay photographic technique that you want to share with others, send it to Joe (*jt@sinclair.com*). If it is appropriate to put it in our next eBay photography book, we will do so and give you the credit.

Recently Joe started a new website, BaysideBusiness, at *http://baysidebusiness.com*. Although it will take several years to reach its potential, Joe intends it to be a place where eBay retailers can go to get a great variety of information on eBay business, ecommerce, and other relevant topics intended to help you achieve success online. It will have a decidedly business flavor to it. And it will include links to resources useful for all eBay businesspeople. It will also eventually include eBay photographic information. So visit BaysideBusiness occasionally to watch the progress.

And good luck with your eBay photography.

Appendix I The Top 12 Tips for Establishing Effective eBay Photography

Top 12 tips for sellers who want to establish high-quality and cost-effective photography for their eBay retail businesses.

1. It's all about light. Think light. Experiment with light. Control light. And your photographic activities will fall into place to create great product photographs.

2. Learn the traditional and digital photography basics. Camera automation cannot completely replace human intelligence and knowledge.

3. Learn to do basic post-processing in Photoshop Elements 3.0 or

the equivalent. It's not difficult. It's fun. And it's necessary for efficient eBay photography.

4. Use batch processing where practical.

5. Understand what kind of photographs eBay buyers need and why. Believe that you can take high-quality photographs that will boost sales.

6. Create advertising photography only in situations where it makes sense. Don't reinvent the wheel; get your advertising displays free from advertisers.

7. You don't need an expensive camera or lots of megapixels to take great product photographs. Most brand-name digital cameras have what it takes.

8. Spend money on professional equipment that creates efficiency. Don't spend money on professional equipment where inexpensive and durable devices make effective substitutes.

9. Plan your studio, work flow, and photograph archives for maximum efficiency and cost-effectiveness. Don't work haphazardously.

10. Always make cost-effectiveness analyses. It's easy to waste too much time and spend too much money on photography.

11. Keep in mind you're not a photographer. You're a businessperson. Shrink the time that you spend taking photographs by carrying through your eBay photographic processes in a smart way.

12. Remember. It's all about light.

Appendix II Useful Technical References

Digital Camera Reviews

Digital Camera Resource, *http://www.dcresource.com*

Digital Photography Review, *http://dpreview.com*

Imaging Resource, *http://www.imaging-resource.com*

Megapixel.net, *http://www.megapixel.net*

Steve's DigiCams, *http://www.steves-digicams.com*

Photography Articles and Tutorials

Building an in-house studio, *http://www.graphic-design.com/photo-graphic/studio*

Build your own photography studio, *http://www.dcmag.co.uk/news/article/mps/UAN/547/v/1/sp/332345698485328313336*

Closeup Photography Lighting, *http://www.cameraontheroad.com/?p=218*

Creating Special Effects in Product Photography, *http://www.webphotoschool.com/Lesson_Library/Free_Lessons/Creating_Special_Effects_in_Product_Photography/*

Dan's Long-Awaited Photo Tutorial-ish Thing, *http://www.dansdata.com/phototute.htm*

Digital Photography How-To: Building a Light Tent, *http://www.creativepro.com/story/feature/19002.html*

Food Photography – How to Take Mouth Watering Photos of Food, *http://www.livingroom.org.au/photolog/tips/food_photography_how_to_take_mouth_watering_photos_of_food.php*

Macro Digital Photography, *http://www.livingroom.org.au/photolog/tips/macro_digital_photography.php*

One Source Lighting: Mimic the Simplicity of the Master, *http://www.alienbees.com/brooksarticle.html*

Photography: Lifestyle vs. Product Shots, *http://catalogagemag.com/mag/marketing_photography_lifestyle_vs/*

Product Photography for Web Designers, *http://www.communitymx.com/abstract.cfm?cid=4280B*

Studio Lighting, *http://www.studiolighting.net/Studio-Lighting-Tutorials.php*

Studio Lighting Accessories, *http://www.vividlight.com/articles/1314.htm*

Tabletop Photography, *http://www.shutterbug.net/features/1003sb_tabletop*

Appendix III Photographic Supplies Resource List

Catalogs and Websites

Adorama, *http://www.adorama.com*

Amvona, *http://www.amvona.com*

B&H Photo-Video-Audio, *http://www.bhphotovideo.com*

Bogen Imaging, *http://www.bogenimaging.us*

Calumet, *http://www.calumetphoto.com*

Freestyle Photographic Supplies, *http://www.freestylephoto.biz*

Porter's Camera Store, *http://porters.com*

RitzCamera, *http://ritzcamera.com*

Sell-It-on-the-net, *http://sell-it-on-the-net.com*

Equipment Marketplaces

Craig's List, *http://www.craigslist.org*

eBay, *http://www.ebay.com*

Froogle, *http://froogle.google.com*

Light Boxes

Photosimile, *http://www.ortery.com*

Litestage, *http://www.litestage.com*

MK Digital Direct, *http://www.mkdigitaldirect.com*

Manikins

Aafiber, *http://www.aafiber.com*

MannequinStore, *http://www.mannequinstore.com*

Photo Archive Software and Services

ACDSee, *http://www.acdsystems.com*

Auction management software (often included)

Celum Imagine, *http://www.celumimagine.com/en*

Image editors (often included)

Picasa, *http://www.picasa.com*

VeriPic Digital Photo Lab, *http://www.veripic.com*

Webshots, *http://webshots.com*

Tents

Alzo, *http://alzodigital.com*

EZcube, *http://www.tabletopstudio.com*

CloudDome, *http://clouddome.com*

Glossary

The following words are used the following ways in this book:

Aspect Ratio The ratio between the width and the height of a photograph. Keep it constant when you resize, or you will get distortion.

Color Temperature The measure of the color of a light source in degrees Kelvin. It measures the relative intensity of blue to red. Incandescent lights (2600K to 3400K) have a yellowish color while a bright sky out of the sun (11000K) has a bluish color.

Cost-Effectiveness Efficient and productive use of your time and your money in regard to your photographic workflow.

Datafeed An exportation of a subset of data from a database to an online marketplace (e.g., Froogle). The subset of data needs to include URLs for the product photographs required for Froogle catalog entries.

Depth of Field The zone in which a subject is in focus. If the subject is too close or too far away, it will be out of the depth of field and out of focus. An open aperture (e.g., f2.8) has a shallow (small) depth of field. A smaller aperture (e.g., f11) has a larger depth of field. A wide angle lens has a larger depth of field than a telephoto lens.

Diffused Light Light that is diffused by something between the light source and the subject (e.g., cloud overcast between the sun and the subject).

Post-Processing The digital processing you do in Adobe Photoshop Elements 3.0, or comparable software, to adjust a photograph to improve its quality and usefulness to prospective buyers. Of course, you do this after you take your photograph, thus the term "post."

Intense Specular Highlights The white spots, burned-out spots, or glare in a photograph caused by too much reflection from a lighting source, which tend to destroy the details of a photograph and make it less useful to prospective buyers.

Workflow The procedures for processing digital photographs individually or in bulk. The workflow consists of systematically taking the photographs and thereafter systematically processing them in an image editor, if necessary.

Index